SERMONS OF GRACE

Sermons from Grace Episcopal
Church in Charleston, South
Carolina, 2012-2014

THE REVEREND JOHN A. ZAHL

The sermons contained herein do not now, nor have ever had any connection, affiliation, or sponsorship with any of the author(s), artist(s), or publications quoted or referenced herein. The content is intended for the purpose of commentary, study, discussion, literary and religious critique.

SERMONS OF GRACE

Published by John Zahl.

Copyright © 2014 by John Zahl.

Cover illustration by Annie vonRosenberg.

Printed in the United States of America

First Edition: October, 2014.

ISBN-13: 978-1503181021

ISBN-10: 1503181022

CONTENTS

Dedicated to the people of Grace Church (Charleston), who picked me up, dusted me off and gave me a front-row pew. I am forever grateful. JAZ+

PREFACE

I write to commend to you this great collection of sermons by my brother priest and friend, John Zahl. It has been my joy to hear these sermons 'live' as John offered them at Grace Church, Charleston.

John's great gift to the Ministry of the Word is surely his gift of connection:

John's connection with a congregation seeking the good news where they live and move and have their being;

John's connection with the Holy Scriptures as he works to make each passage come alive in the here and now world of the listener;

John's connection with a God whom we can know daily by no better name than love and grace.

I pray that these sermons will speak to you as they have already spoken to so many. Let them wash over you and help to change the very place where you now dwell, and may you know it anew as a place of ever-revealing grace.

Faithfully,

Michael+
The Reverend Canon J. Michael A. Wright
Rector of Grace Church

SERMONS OF GRACE
(AN INTRODUCTION)

Preaching is the act of trying to connect people to God and God to people. More than that, it is especially designed to help the sufferer. The message may not promise relief from the rut, but it certainly can reorient the perspective of the one who is feeling paralyzed. At least, that is the hope.

Each of these sermons begins with the assumption that God has accomplished something on Calvary that makes a difference in life. It reflects the movement of God, as opposed to the movement of the self. Martin Luther went so far as to posit, "any philosophy of life that points a person toward an inward solution produces despair." Regardless of whether or not he was right about all cases, Christian hope, when offered in such a way that it leaves little room for the agency of the recipient, stands in high relief against the backdrop of all suggestions that "something (else) needs to be done."

The Gospel, in other words, brings comfort by speaking to us from outside of ourselves, beyond our hopes, fears, and efforts, reminding us that God is trustworthy and ultimately sufficient.

In my own attempts to convey this Gospel, I rely upon a few themes, many of them taken loosely from a Lutheran understanding of preaching. For those familiar with that tradition, the message of God's grace is each sermon's final destination. Grace, in other words, is the subtext that underpins each and every one of them.

From the outset, the intention is to winsomely expose some chink in our armor, some aspect of our lives which is not as we wish it to be. This is "the Law," and in preaching that means the contrast between the ideal of God's Law and our own less-than-ideal lives. The Lectionary selections usually provide an avenue by which to reveal our vulnerability, exposing parts of life with which we all struggle.

I have become convinced that such vulnerability finds its first valuable expression in the life of the preacher. If this is true, then perhaps effective preaching depends heavily upon a pastor's personal experience with the theological material. One preacher, Nadia Bolz-Weber, described this principle in a recent interview: "As a preacher, *I* have to go through a process of being convicted of something in the text. *I* have to somehow suffer that text myself in order to have anything to say about it."

In Thomas Melanchthon's *Loci Communes* (1521), he wrote that "the heart and its affections must be the highest and most powerful part of man." It's an empirically evident assertion: the inner person is directed primarily by desire and not thought. Accordingly, these sermons seek to target the emotional life of the reader. My best ally in this undertaking has been stories, both from fiction and from real life. I hope these illustrations bring the ideas to life. Communicating Biblical ideas to the hearts of an audience requires as much, and I rely upon heart-felt illustrations in order to do this. In short, illustrations take the message and (*via* the mind) introduce it to the soul. As the Irish priest's daughter says to her father in the film *Calvary*, "*your words are corny… but I like them.*"

Sermons of grace probe the problematic aspects of life in an attempt to apply compassion. Our hearts are often reluctant, but it is there that the Gospel message meets us. I hope these sermons can help by reevaluating our felt needs and by absolving our conscious (and unconscious) guilt. Ideally, one leaves church feeling that some important aspect of her life has been accurately addressed, and in that place, she has encountered a love which enables her to face the coming week with confidence.

It is worth noting that the entire flow of Sunday morning liturgy found in *The Book of Common Prayer*, which so profoundly orients the tradition of Episcopalian worship, also aims to address us where we are and there provide absolution. The sermon offers nothing more than that which is being conveyed through the sacraments. As Thomas Cranmer put it, "For as the word of God preached putteth Christ into our ears; so likewise these elements of water, bread, and wine, joined to God's word, do, after a sacramental manner, put Christ into our eyes, mouths, hands, and all our senses." Their object and substance, in other words, are identical. Only the medium differs. John Hooper echoed this view when he wrote of the Holy Communion as "*a visible word that preacheth* peace between God and man." We see this depicted beautifully in one of the stained-glass windows here at Grace Church. It features only a Bible and a chalice, the two grouped together as complementary expressions of the church's ministry: "the Word preached and the sacrament duly administered." This volume is a simple effort to bring home the power of the former.

May the words of my mouth and the meditations of our hearts be always acceptable in Thy sight, O Lord, our strength and our redeemer. Amen.

Rev. John Zahl
Grace Church, Charleston
The Feast of the Holy Cross, 2014

Are You Ready for Anything?
(December 1, 2013)

"Prepare the way of the Lord..." (Matthew 3:3)

John the Baptist's words this morning are unequivocal: *"Prepare ye the way of the Lord."* It is undeniable that "preparation" is one of the main themes of Advent.

The readings in Advent contain an eschatological emphasis, which means that they deal with the final events of history and the anticipation of that which has not yet happened. They prepare us for Christmas by positioning us to look ahead with anticipation. We await the breaking-in of God into our midst, and we savor the coming of Christ. The mood is one of excitement about something that is about to happen.

I spoke yesterday with a friend whose wife is about to have a baby. They're due in just a few weeks. They have come through a long period of preparation, and now, in just days, their entire life together is going to change dramatically. As one person put it, you'll love having a child so long as you're "cool with everything changing." I asked my buddy: "So what's your state of mind, now that you are in the final countdown of the last few days?" His answer was perfect: "honestly, I'm just excited."

So it's appropriate then for me to ask you a question which is probably already present in your thinking, especially since Thanksgiving has been over for almost three days: "Are you ready for Christmas?" "Are you ready yet?"

In my experience, asking a person if they are "ready" (for anything) almost always brings anxiety to the surface. I experienced this somewhat tragically one Saturday evening as I was waiting in line for the procession into my ordination to the Deaconate. I mentioned to a fellow clergyman that my Rector had given me the honor of allowing me to be the preacher at all of the Sunday services the next day. To this, the clergy friend responded: "Ooh that's great. You're preaching at all three services tomorrow. Wow! Are you ready?"

I immediately felt my level of anxiety rise. I think I said, "pretty much," but in truth, his asking me that one question completely undid my confidence. It drew to the surface a feeling of not being at all ready. It's embarrassing to admit that as I knelt down to have the Bishop lay his hands on me, I was not exactly awash in feelings of holiness and gratitude. Instead, my mind kept flashing back to spiteful thoughts about the clergyman who had asked me that question.

The question of readiness has this vexing power. Not only does it undo us. It also causes in us this weird desire to kind of scramble, a sudden need to jump into whatever it is that is left undone. It inspires in us this need to tackle the remainder of whatever it is that we feel unprepared for, and it causes us to sense that our efforts will possibly not be enough. It causes us to sense either that there's not enough time left, or that we are full of deep-seated impatience.

Advent is, in part, designed to do exactly that. It draws attention to our impatience. It forces us to reflect upon the fact that we're not all that good at waiting. We would much rather pounce than pause. I suspect that many of you will now leave the service early, right after communion, just so that you can get an early start on the rest of your day.

Earlier this week I was reading an article by a psychiatrist who wrote extensively during the middle part of the 20th century, named Dr. Harry Tiebout. He specialized in the psychology of the mind in relationship to ideas of surrender. In a paper entitled, "The Act of Surrender in the Therapeutic Process," he wrote at some length about the infantile origins of impatience in the human psyche. Listen to this quote:

> "[Another] significant aspect of the child's original psyche is its tendency to do everything in a hurry. Observe youngsters on the beach: they run rather than walk. Observe them coming on a visit: the younger ones tear from the car while their elder siblings adopt a more leisurely pace. The three-year-olds, and more so the twos, cannot engage in play requiring long periods of concentration. Whatever they are doing must be done quickly. As the same children age, they gradually become able to stick to one activity for longer times... Thus at the start of life the psyche cannot accept frustrations, and func-

tions at a tempo allegretto with a good deal of staccato and vivace thrown in.

"Now the question is, 'If the infantile psyche persists into adult life, how will its presence be manifested?' In general, when infantile traits continue into adulthood, the person is spoken of as immature... It is youth that drives fast, thinks fast, feels fast, moves fast, acts hastily in most situations. *There can be little question that one of the hallmarks of the immature is the proneness to be under inner pressure for accomplishment.* Big plans, big schemes, big hopes abound, unfortunately not matched by an ability to produce.

As I read those words, I can't help but think of my one-year-old daughter, Daphne. My inability to microwave instant oatmeal at a speed that is to her liking is often the cause of great alarm. But I too identify with the doctor's description. I wonder if his words, written in 1953, accurately describe a bit of your personality. Do you know what it's like to do things hastily in an attempt to achieve full realization of the big picture? Do you know what it's like to try to claw your way back to the top of your to-do list with a kind of frenzied intensity?

Well, we're meant to consider these aspects of life during Advent. It is a time when we confront our feelings of un-readiness and impatience. It's also a time when we look at all the ways in which life seems constantly to be frustrating our attempts at control. Let's face it: having to wait for things is a huge part of life. And it is a part of life that, to us, feels wrong.

Is there something that you are being forced to wait for? A friend wrote the following comment on her Facebook page this past Friday: *"Comcast's Black Friday Special: Extra slow internet at your regular rate, all day long!"* She certainly knows what it is like to wait.

Sure, there's waiting for the internet to speed up. But there's also waiting for an acceptance letter... waiting for school to be over... waiting to meet the right person... waiting for a baby to be born... there's waiting for jobs... waiting for houses to sell... waiting for traffic... even (sometimes) waiting for loved ones to die.

Life is full of waiting, and ultimately, control is not the answer. After all, it's acceptance of our lack of control that reminds us who we are, even who God has made us to be.

It is good for us to have to wait. Waiting is okay. It is underrated. It is not a sign of punishment or of failure or of wrongdoing.

I encountered this profoundly when I lived in New York City many years ago. I was part of a small Bible study. At the end of our time together each week, we would say a few prayers for each other. One of our members, Tom, offered the same prayer request every week. He said he hated his job, and he wanted us to pray that God would give him a new one. So we did this. Every week, one of us would remind God that Tom was miserable in his work, and then we would ask him to give Tom a new job. This went on for two years, until one day, a new guy joined our group.

When it came time for prayer requests, this friend, Dan, offered to pray. We explained how Tom hates his job and how every week we ask God to give Tom a new job…

Dan proceeded to pray a most audacious prayer. He said:

> "Dear Lord, we thank You for Tom's current job. Help him to accept that this is the place You have currently chosen for him. Show him how he can be helpful there and, if it be Your will, provide him with a new opportunity when the time is right. Amen."

We were flabbergasted! But Dan was right on the money.

A few weeks later, Tom told us that he had received a frantic call from his boss one evening, that he desperately needed Tom's help with a last-minute presentation. Tom showed up to bail his boss out, and the two worked late into the night together alone in the office. At the end of the evening, the man thanked him sincerely. Then he proceeded to open up to Tom about some personal concerns which had been eating away at him. Tom was able to empathize and listen. He had been given an opportunity to convey compassion to a guy who was in need of it. Tom felt in some weird way that this had been an answer to Dan's prayer. What's more, a few months later Tom was offered a new job, and he was able to move out of the stagnant situation.

If you are being made to wait in some aspect of your life right now, know this morning that God is in that place with you, like a quiet friend in a waiting room, patiently holding out with you, there to share with you in the excitement of what will finally arrive, and also to help you get through this time of passivity without tearing all of your hair out. For unlike you, He *is* good at waiting, and He is as patient as you need Him to be.

Ultimately, I believe that waiting and hoping are basically synonymous terms. Where there is waiting, there is hope. *Amen.*

A FRIEND IN THE RAIN
(CHRISTMAS EVE, 2013)

"This will be a sign for you: you will find a child wrapped in bands of cloth and lying in a manger." (Luke 2:12)

Picture two lines, one horizontal and the other vertical. Now imagine the two lines crossing each other, coming together at a single point of intersection. Christmas is about the place where human life intersects with the divine, the place where the two connect.

The Christmas story draws us back to that famous moment in history when God entered into our midst in the form of a newborn infant. Think about that image with me for a moment. Picture the tiny Christ child, peacefully lying in the manger in the cold of night. If this is anything, it is an image of gentleness, of compassion, and of grace. And it comes without an ounce of judgment. One might even go so far as to suggest that God is an Otis Redding fan, or at least a fan of that classic song: "Try a Little Tenderness."

Almost two years ago, I took my baby daughter to a retirement home to visit some of the elderly folks there and to join me for our weekly communion service. One of the women there, named Nancy, was dealing with the realities of Alzheimer's… and she kept getting up from her seat because she wanted to hold Daphne. Daphne was completely fine with it, but it disrupted our service a little bit. We ended up having Nancy sit next to me so that she could hold Daphne's hand.

Nancy taught me about Christmas and about what it meant that God chose to reveal Himself to us in the form of the Christ child. It is an endlessly powerful symbol, one to which we cannot help but respond, and it draws us in.

There is a wonderful psychologist who lives in Houston, Texas, named Brené Brown. She also happens to be an Episcopalian. In a recent RSA animated short, she spoke about the importance of empathy when dealing with folks who are going through a tough time. She reported—what you already know, I'm sure—that people often don't respond to others with empathy. Much more common, for example, is advice-giving, or a distanced form of sympathy. Brown says that people dealing with difficulty often feel removed from their fellow human beings, like they're down in a hole. She describes the ways that people often interact with them.

They might say, "How can you feel bad when it's so beautiful outside? The weather's great up here." They talk down to you, looking into your little hole from above. You say, "I had a miscarriage." They respond, "At least you know you can get pregnant." You say, "My son is flunking out of school." They say, "at least your daughter is a straight-A student." At least, at least, at least...

The empathetic response, on the other hand, chooses to make itself vulnerable. It climbs down into the hole and sits next to you. It might not say a word, but it is there. It identifies and it listens.

As Brown puts it, empathy is so important because when people are hurting, they are not typically helped by "a *response*." What they need is "a *connection*."

I heard of a profound expression of this kind of response just recently. One of my friends, also a psychologist, works at a V.A. (Veterans Affairs) hospital. He specializes in treating patients who are suffering from Post-Traumatic Stress Disorder, mostly men and women who have spent time overseas, in places like Afghanistan. Many of them have come home in rough shape, often struggling with the ability just to leave their apartment, to integrate with people. One of the typical symptoms is extreme paranoia—constantly looking over one's shoulder—which usually results in severe agoraphobia.

My friend uses a form of cognitive behavioral therapy that works remarkably well, called exposure therapy. It involves exposing the patients to the things they are afraid of through a slow, progressive process. For most of these folks, it involves spending time around people, crowds and strangers. They'll start by riding in an elevator, and then, for example, build to taking a trip to Wal-Mart.

One of the guys whom my friend was working with was a vet who could barely leave his apartment when they began the treatment. After the gentleman had made substantial headway in their session, he agreed to attend a River-dogs baseball game at Joe Riley stadium down the street. He would sit in the bleachers in the middle of a crowd full of strangers for a prolonged period of time, and he would try to enjoy himself. It would be a big step for him.

When the day arrived, he went up and nervously bought a ticket. He made it to his seat and sat down just as the game was beginning. All was going well, but then something horrible happened. The heavens opened, and it started to rain. It started to pour. And everybody climbed up out of the bleachers, and they all ran to the top of the steps, where they huddled together like sardines under an overstretched awning to stay dry.

But this poor guy, he looked up and saw everybody squished together, and it was too much for him to bear. He couldn't do it. And so he sat there in the rain, paralyzed and getting drenched.

Now here's the crazy part. Bill Murray, the famous actor and comedian—probably the most well-loved across-the-board celebrity that there is—happens to be a part owner of the Riverdogs, and he was there that night. Bill Murray looked down from his box and saw this fellow sitting in the rain alone in the bleachers getting drenched. And then Bill Murray did an amazing thing. He went down in the middle of the rainstorm and sat down next to the guy, and he said, "Hello. What's going on?"

And the guy completely opened up. He said, "I'm here... I'm a veteran... I can't go up there... P.T.S.D.... Oh my gosh, you're Bill Murray!... Afghanistan... etc."

As the guy tells it, it was the best moment of his life. And Bill Murray saw to it that he got season tickets. He said, "Why don't you watch the next game from up in my box?" And he befriended him.

This is the kind of love that the Gospel speaks of: the God of the universe is not just all-powerful and likeable, but He actually likes *you*. And He has come down to engage with you there, like Bill Murray, in effect, but even better, as a friend who is committed to seeing you through.

Christmas is our reminder that God has come down from on high, and He has entered into our midst, and His will for us is "good." In other words, *Christ is the empathy of God.*

Think of that feeling you get when you look upon a newborn infant. Christmas reminds us that this is the feeling God has for each of you. *Amen.*

CATCHING FLIES WITH HONEY
(DECEMBER 28, 2014)

"But now that faith has come, we are no longer subject to a disciplinarian..." (Galatians 3:25)

There is a wise old saying that relates to this morning's readings. Perhaps you've heard it before: *"You can catch more flies with honey than with vinegar."* It's an adage suggesting that in life, there are two very distinct approaches to dealing with problems that one can make use of. These are the "honey" approach and the "vinegar" approach.

Obviously, the honey method is sweet and alluring. It lures you in with a sticky embrace. The vinegar method, on the other hand, is sour and intense, and it packs a punch.

Now notice with me where the Gospel writer picks up on a similar theme in his famous prologue. He writes: *"The law indeed was given through Moses; grace and truth came through Jesus Christ."* Here we see what some theologians have described as the two primary, overarching themes of the entire Bible, two voices woven throughout the whole of Scripture, commonly known as "Law" and "Gospel." For this morning's purposes, we can equate "Law" with "vinegar" and "Gospel" with "honey." They map onto each other rather well.

We find the same material present in this morning's Epistle. St. Paul writes: "The law was our disciplinarian until Christ came." He contrasts a "disciplinarian" (the Law) with "Christ" (who is the perfect expression of grace).

It makes sense then for us to give a little thought to these two distinct voices. I wish to do so not just because I find these ideas to be practically popping out of the readings, but mainly because they are themes which run throughout the fabric of our lives. We encounter them at every turn.

Are you familiar, for example, with "the Law," with the "vinegar" side of life, which is a voice full of "discipline?" It wants the best for you. It seeks to help. It is the voice of all "good advice."

Perhaps you've encountered the Law written with a capital "L," like in the famous form of the Ten Commandments. "Thou shalt not covet." "*No* idols"! "Do not steal!"

I think it's fair to say that they, in and of themselves, are not words that ooze comfort. They don't sound much like honey, do they? *The Book of Common Prayer* is right to remind us that a good way to respond to such exhortations is with that classic three-word phrase: "Lord, have mercy."

Or maybe you've encountered the law written with a medium-sized "L." "No speeding." "No shirt and shoes, no service." Or even, "What colleges did *your* kids get into?" It is the voice of society, its standards and expectations. I saw a good example of this in yesterday's Washington Post, in an article about Chinese parents. Its headline: "China Passes Law Requiring People to Visit Their Elderly Parents or Risk Being Sued by Them." The reporter writes:

> "BEIJING — Visit your parents. That's an order. So says China, whose national legislature on Friday amended its law on the elderly to require that adult children visit their aged parents 'often'—or risk being sued by them. The amendment does not specify how frequently such visits should occur. State media say the new clause will allow elderly parents who feel neglected by their children to take them to court."

I have not found that lawsuits typically strengthen bonds among kin. In fact, it seems to me that exactly the opposite is the case. Has a friend or family member ever given you a guilt trip? If you really want to alienate a family member, I recommend taking them to court.

We encounter medium-sized "L" law all the time. Often, it comes from the people we are closest to. I saw this portrayed devastatingly in a movie called *Spanglish*, in a scene in which a mother, played by Tia Leoni, buys her daughter a new wardrobe. At first the daughter is so excited, but then she realizes that none of the clothes will fit her until she loses 20 pounds.

And there is also a lower-case "l" law. It's what happens when everyone else's expectations become internalized. It's the subtlest form of all, because it's usually left unspoken. I'm talking about the law that lives in-between your ears. This is the law that you hold over your own head, like a guillotine. "I'm not *blank* enough... I need to be more *blank*," and all of the other "*shoulds.*" Freud called it the "super-ego."

Perhaps this version of the law is especially present this week, since New Year's Eve is right around the corner. May I ask, have you come up with any fresh New Year's resolutions for 2013? Are you about to take on the role of "disciplinarian," once and for all, for yourself? Not to be a cynic, but I wonder how well it all will go. Have you ever tried making similar changes before? In my own case, I find that the majority of my resolutions revisit me on a yearly basis, like old friends with whom I'm about to become reacquainted. *"Time to re-join the gym... and no more pizza."*

When the law takes a front row seat in our lives, two things happen. Either we become completely fixated upon our adherence to it, getting mean or passive-aggressive with anyone who doesn't feel the same way about our regime. Or, more typically, *we just become discouraged.*

The law exhausts us and taxes us. It demands a pound of flesh. And so St. Paul calls it a "disciplinarian" and "a letter that kills" and even "a ministration of death." I think it's high time we discuss the other voice, the honey-like voice that is "grace."

In a little-known short story by George Elliot called *Janet's Repentance*, we learn of a sweet woman named Janet, who is on the verge of a nervous breakdown. In a very low moment she remembers meeting a nice, young clergyman named Mr. Tryan. The author describes her train of thought:

> "...But there was one spot in her memory which seemed
> to promise her an untried spring, where the waters

might be sweet. That short meeting with Mr. Tryan had come back upon her—his voice, his words, his look, which told her that he knew sorrow. ... surely he knew more of the secrets of sorrow than other men; perhaps he had some message of comfort, different from the feeble words she had been used to hearing from others. She was tired, she was sick of that barren exhortation—Do right, and keep a clear conscience. She wanted strength to do right—she wanted something to rely on besides her own resolutions; for was not the path behind her all strewn with broken resolutions? How could she trust in new ones? She had often heard Mr. Tryan laughed at for being fond of great sinners. She began to see a new meaning in those words; he would perhaps understand her helplessness..."

The second voice is the voice of Mr. Tryan. It is the Gospel voice, the *final* voice. Writer Steve Brown tells the story of a boy who encounters the law:

"[There was] a little boy who killed his grandmother's pet duck. He accidentally hit the duck with a rock from his sling-shot. The boy didn't think anybody saw him do it, so he buried the duck in the backyard and didn't tell a soul.

"Later, the boy found out that his sister had seen it all. And she now had the leverage of his secret and used it against him. Whenever it was the sister's turn to wash the dishes, take out the garbage, or wash the car, she would whisper in his ear, 'Remember the duck.' And then the little boy would do whatever chore his sister was supposed to be doing. 'Remember the duck. Remember the duck...'

"But there is always a limit to that sort of thing. Finally he'd had it. The boy went to his grandmother and, with great fear, confessed what he had done. *To his surprise, she hugged him and thanked him. She said, "I was standing at the kitchen sink and saw the whole thing. I forgave you then. I was just wondering when you were going to get tired of your sister's blackmail and come to me."*

Just like that grandmother's voice, grace absorbs the accusation of the law. The law prepares our hearts to hear good news, but then grace trumps it, for grace is a voice that subsumes the law. Unlike the law, it is tender, enabling, and totally sufficient. It is the end of all scorekeeping. It forgives trespasses, saying, *"Neither do I condemn thee."*

To quote St. Paul again from another portion of this morning's Epistle, "now that faith has come, we are no longer subject to a disciplinarian." In short, God is not a disciplinarian. *Amen.*

I KNOW WHERE I'M GOING
(JANUARY 6, 2013)

"They set out; and there, ahead of them, went the star..."
(Matt 2:9)

This morning we celebrate Epiphany. We remember the star that led the three wise men to the little baby Jesus. And so it is, too, that we reflect upon God's guidance in the midst of life.

One needs only to read the story recounted in this morning's Gospel to conclude that these three men were incredibly wise, for they followed God's prompting and were (by His grace) able to set out in hope and trust, and with great courage, into the unknown. And they were not disappointed with what they found.

Of course, you could also argue that they were incredibly *un*wise, setting off into the unknown with a poorly thought-out plan. (Pointing into the distance), "Let's follow that star to see where it will lead us." You see, they did not know exactly where they were heading. But they set out nonetheless.

The whole idea, when you think about it, sounds almost... *foolish.*

On a related note, there is a wonderful movie named *I Know Where I'm Going* that came out in 1946. It was directed by the famous team of Powell and Pressburger, who were kind of the like the UK's answer to America's Frank Capra.

In *I Know Where I'm Going*, we follow the story of a bright and beautiful young woman named Joan Webster. She is eager to leave behind her "middle-class" upbringing and seeks to marry a man of substantial means. When she tells her father the news that she is about to marry Sir Robert Bellinger, she also shares with him her guiding dictum, a tag line which she repeats throughout the film: "I know where I'm going," she says.

And she says it over and over again, when she boards the train bound for Scotland, where she is to be married on the Island of Kiloran to the famous industrialist. "I know where I'm going." She says it when she arrives on the nearby island of Mull, just a short boat ride away from Kiloran. "I know where I'm going."

But then a huge storm front moves in. It enshrouds the island in fog and makes it impossible for her to finish the journey. Twice she sets off by herself stubbornly in a dingy, once into the fog and a second time into a terrible storm. She has to be rescued and brought back to Mull both times.

It's a story that offers a true portrait of life. The more Joan Webster says, "I know where I'm going," the more we realize that, in fact, she does not know where she is going. And that's what makes the movie so much fun to watch, all these years later, because, as is the case also with this morning's two thousand year-old reading, the story of life in this regard has not changed one iota.

We do not and cannot know exactly where we are going. That, you see, is where God comes in. This is the wisdom of the wise men: they did not know where they were going (and they knew it)! But they trusted God, who did, and followed His lead.

My friend and fellow Episcopal clergyman R-J Heijmen puts it like this:

> "In our constant quest for happiness, for peace, the an-
> swer is to be found not in the quest for control, but in
> the release of it...As we walk through life, constantly
> frustrated by our inability to be and do what we want,
> the answer is not self-mastery, but rather the love of the
> Master"

...which is the guidance of God, the Good Shepherd.

A friend of mine, who is a Christian, went through a rough time some years ago, and found himself having to enter the fellowship of Alcoholics Anonymous. He was dismayed at first when he encountered their famous slogan: "One Day at a Time." He was convinced that such a laissez-faire phi-losophy would prevent anything of substance from taking form in his life. How would he arrive at any of his goals if he disregarded the future and only focused on the 24 hours in front of him?

Then a savvy AA old-timer asked him if he had a relative-ly clear idea about what the rest of the day would require of him. The newcomer, my buddy, said he did and rattled off a list of a few errands, a meal, a phone call, and some TV before bed. The wise old-timer responded: "Then you see, *you do know* what God's will is for you. It will unfold best if you just allow God to guide you, *one day at a time*." It's a train of thought which Jesus himself affirmed. He famously called it "daily bread."

Today's Gospel offers us a beautiful description of this type of approach, and it is one that encapsulates, to a large extent, the way of faith.

"They set out; and there, ahead of them, went the star that they had seen at its rising, until it stopped over the place where the child was. When they saw that the star had stopped, they were overwhelmed with joy."

We do well to pause this morning, to ask ourselves: "Do I think that I know where I'm going?" and, even more importantly, to ask God: "Will you guide us? Help us to get to the places where we are going, which are, in fact, the places where we will find You."

Let us close with this morning's Collect:

"O God, by the leading of a star you manifested your only Son to the peoples of the earth: Lead us, who know you now by faith, to your presence, where we may see your glory face to face; through Jesus Christ our Lord, who lives and reigns with you and the Holy Spirit, one God, now and for ever. *Amen.*"

The Lesson of the Silent Women
(January 30, 2013)

"Because he himself was tested by what he suffered, he is able to help those who are being tested." (Hebrews 2:18)

This is a poignant passage, one that drips with compassion. But not only does it provide comfort; it actually helps to *explain comfort*. "Because he himself was tested by what he suffered, he is able to help those who are being tested." Here we read that God himself knows what it means to suffer.

We see this theme writ large in the life of Christ. In this respect, you can almost feel the Lenten season barreling toward us. Jesus suffered. Jesus was tested by adversity and abandonment. Life for him was not always easy, which is an understatement.

And is this not also true for us, at least some of the time? Are there not times when we wish that people would be honest for a moment about how hard it can be just to make it from one long day to the next? Can we not wipe the smiles from our faces for a second, so that we may acknowledge our

41

struggles? Or are we never allowed to be sad and tired?

Well, tonight we are reminded that the Church is no stranger to hardship. Our faith often comes to bear most profoundly in our lives in the places that are rough. I am not talking about dwelling on frustrations, but I am talking about identifying with them. Because, you see, God identifies with us, with you and me, right smack dab in the middle of *real* life.

It is in that identification that we realize just how much God cares for us. I don't want to overstate things, but it's fair to say that a huge percentage of meaningful ministry comes from the place where identification is found. I'm referring to shared experience, which quickly translates into understanding (a.k.a. empathy), which, to my way of thinking, greatly resembles love.

It's no surprise that the finest grief counselors have themselves usually been through terrible losses. That often the most patient and wisest nurses have themselves experienced illness and surgery and the need for care. I have, for example, seen widows counsel other widows in a way that I could never do.

A beautiful illustration of this comes from a Japanese movie that was made in the mid-80s by the famous director Akira Kurosawa. The film is called *Rhapsody in August.* In it we encounter an elderly lady who has agreed to look after her grandchildren for the summer. It is quickly made known to the viewer that this admirable woman lost her husband tragically in the bombing of Hiroshima.

One day, in the middle of the afternoon, her grand-children spot an older lady walking up the driveway to the house. She is greeted by the grandmother and ushered into the living room, where the two women sit down across from each other, facing one another. The grandchildren watch the scene, peering through the slats in the parlor door. They re-mark to each other: "Why aren't they saying anything?", for the two women are seen sitting there without so much as a single word being uttered between them.

After about an hour of sitting in complete silence, the visitor gets up and leaves the house. When she is gone, the children ask their grandmother, "Who was that woman? And why didn't the two of you say anything to each other?"

The grandmother replies: *"She too lost her husband to the bomb. So we don't have to say anything to each other in order to say what needs to be said."*

And so it is with compassion. Identification is a crucial ingredient. It reminds us that we are not alone. It helps to lift the burdens from each other's backs, and it reminds us that there are those who went before us who functioned in the same way in our own lives.

I wonder, this evening, have you been given a hard-earned avenue to compassion through your experience of life? I pray that God will enable you to make use of it.

And please don't forget that God himself has been to the depths of experience too. He is often found precisely in those places, not just in *your* life, but in the life of the world. God has identified with us in Christ, reminding us of the extent of His love for us and ability to understand whatever it is that we are going through, even this week, on a Wednesday night on Wentworth Street. *May our difficulties, if nothing else, not be for nothing. Amen.*

An Old Man and a Baby
(February 2, 2014)

Dedicated to Fr. Joseph A. DiRaddo

"This child is destined... to be a sign that will be opposed so that the inner thoughts of many will be revealed..."
(Luke 2:34-25)

Today we remember Simeon, a man after whom my brother is named, so obviously I'm a fan of this story. In it we see all of life, the elderly and the newborn, the wise and the innocent. This famous encounter between old Simeon and the baby Jesus is portrayed beautifully above the altar in the chapel at Bishop Gadsden retirement community on James Island. It is one of my favorite paintings in Charleston.

So what do we learn from it? Simeon had enough insight to see, in this baby, the dawn of a new era. He was able to anticipate the significance and impact that this one child would have upon the history of the world. He spoke these famous words (known as the *nunc dimittis*):

"Lord, now lettest thou thy servant depart in peace, according to thy word. For mine eyes have seen thy salvation..."

But he also spoke some slightly less famous words to the child's mother, and it's upon them that I wish to focus our attention this morning. He said:

"This child is destined... to be a sign that will be opposed so that the inner thoughts of many will be revealed..."

We hear in them that Simeon not only anticipated the profoundly positive impact that Jesus would have upon the world; he also saw that the Gospel message, of which the Christ child was the embodiment, would arouse "opposition," that the grace of God would "reveal" in human hearts a certain ambivalence to the movement of the Spirit.

What is this "opposition" to which Simeon refers? Do you remember the parable of the Laborers in the Vineyard? In it Jesus tells the story of a vineyard owner who hires workers at multiple points during the workday. Some of them begin their work early in the morning, others in the middle of the day, while others work only a short hour or two. At the end of the workday, the owner generously pays them all the same, full day's wage. Matthew tells us about the reaction of those who worked longest:

"And when they received it, they grumbled against the landowner, saying, 'These last worked only one hour, and you have made them equal to us who have borne the burden of the day and the scorching heat.'"

46

Or perhaps you remember a similar response from the Parable of the Prodigal Son. When the older brother hears that his wild and wasteful younger brother's return has been viewed as a cause for celebration (and not serious restitution), he is furious and refuses to have anything to do with the proceedings.

Simeon's word "opposition" is not too strong. If anything, it's too mild. It was a response to Jesus' ministry that followed him everywhere he went, so much so that, in the end, it crystallized into the form of a kind of conspiracy. The forgiveness of sins which Christ demonstrated so powerfully (again and again), ultimately got him crucified. By many, you see, such an approach was understood to be a threat. In theological terms, this response has traditionally been referred to as: "the offense of the Gospel." To let miscreants off the hook seems to be frightfully irresponsible, not to mention unfair.

The late Robert Capon puts a congregational voice to this complaint:

> "Restore to us, Preacher, the comfort of merit and demerit. But do not preach us grace. It will not do to split the pot evenly at four in the morning and break out the Chivas Regal. We insist on being reckoned with. Give us something, anything; but spare us the indignity of this indiscriminate acceptance" (*Between Noon and Three*, p 8).

Of course, to others—and perhaps even to you—the forgiveness of sins is a message that carries with it hope and reconciliation, and a way out of all that binds and burdens us. The prophet Anna (who is mentioned at the end of our Gospel lesson as one who was very much on Simeon's same wave-length) summarized its impact in a single word: *"re-demption."*

In the Christmas episode that closed out the first season of the British television show, *Call the Midwife*, a poignant illustration of these two responses is found in the account of a young teenage mother who conceals her pregnancy from her parents. She manages to give birth to the child in secret, but then suffers complications that require medical attention. The baby is left with the midwives as the young girl undergoes surgery.

When the parents realize what has happened, they are mortified and ashamed. In an offhand remark, her father mentions that he "is a church warden, and her mum is the head of the Women's Guild." They plan to have the child adopted quietly, and then to bury the issue completely from memory.

But when the time comes for the mother of the child to sign the adoption papers, the parents accompany her to Nonnatus House, where the midwives are caring for the infant in the interim. They allow the young mother, against her parents' wishes, to see her baby. The poor girl cries as she holds her little one for the last time, with the parents looking on in the background. She says, "I'm so sorry," to which her mother responds: "Well, it's too late for that, isn't it?" But her father nudges his wife, and says, "She's not saying it to us. She's telling it to the baby."

Then the girl's parents gather behind her. For the first time, they set eyes upon their grandchild. In that short moment, their hearts melt within them. They decide, instead, to bring the baby home with them and to raise the child as their own. It is an incredibly moving sequence of events. The episode closes a few weeks later with the two moms walking down the street past some neighbors, pushing the basinet together, chatting and smiling. The grandfather donates hay to the nuns for their Christmas pageant. All has been forgiven, and they are better for it.

Perhaps this kind of response is not the best way to deal with trespass. But it *is a way*. I believe it is God's way, and personally, I am most grateful that it is. In truth, whether we like it or not, as a Christian church, we do well to recognize that ultimately, it is also *our way*.

Charles Spurgeon, the famous 19th Century British preacher, put it like this, and I close with his words:

> "My dear Brethren, do not try to make (the Gospel) tasteful to carnal minds. Hide not the offense of the cross, lest you make it of none effect. The angles and corners of the gospel are its strength: to pare them off is to deprive it of power. Toning down is not the increase of strength, but the death of it... If you remove grace out of the gospel, the gospel is gone. If the people do not like the doctrine of grace, give them all the more of it."

Amen.

"THESE GO TO 11"
(FEBRUARY 16, 2014)

"Be perfect, therefore, as your heavenly Father is perfect."
(Matthew 5:48)

A theologian friend of mine once made this comment about
The Sermon on the Mount: "The Sermon on the Mount is
the perfect primer for the Cross." He meant that The Sermon on the Mount sets the stage in such a way that we can
appreciate the events that transpired on Calvary and the significance of the Empty Tomb that followed them. Today I
want to explain the implications of this idea as it relates to
the passage we have been given in this morning's Gospel.

Our reading covers a substantial stretch of Matthew's fifth
chapter, taken from the first third of that famous sermon. It's
easy to argue that this is the greatest sermon ever preached,
by the way. You may be familiar with many bits of it. We get
The Lord's Prayer from it. We get the Beatitudes ("Blessed
are the…") from it. "Love your enemy"—we get that from
it. And many other famous passages of Scripture.

Today I want to focus on how it might have been heard by the listeners themselves, who first heard it live. Imagine, Christ climbs up on top of a mountain, and then proceeds to quote portions of the Ten Commandments after saying: "You have heard it said…" Do you know what that brought to mind for people? He was, without a doubt, referencing Moses. Then he would follow the quoted commandment by saying, "…But I say." He was boldly asserting that he spoke with an authority that rivaled—and even supplanted—that of the greatest hero of the Jewish faith, Moses. He takes Moses' most famous announcement, and then he goes even further with it.

Maybe you remember that all-time classic, the original mockumentary, *This Is Spinal Tap*. In a famous scene, Nigel, the lead guitarist (played brilliantly by Christopher Guest), is being interviewed about his equipment, and he shows the interviewer his beloved amplifiers and points out that the dials on all of his amps—unlike everyone else's—go to "11." He keeps saying, "yeah, but these go to eleven, which is one louder, isn't it?" The Sermon on the Mount kicks off with the Law of Moses at "one louder." He has turned up the volume.

He says, paraphrasing, "You've heard it said, 'Thou shalt not murder.' But I say to you, if you have anger in your heart, it's the same thing… You've heard it said, 'Thou shalt not commit adultery.' But I say to you, if you have lust in your heart, it's the same thing." It's radical stuff, equating lust with adultery, and anger with murder.

And that's not what we usually do, is it? If I'm lying in bed at 11:30, and I manage not to give in to that late night Häagen-Dazs craving, I feel as though I have accomplished something. I wake up in the morning with the sense that I've had some kind of a victory. I haven't, according to this standard.

We live in a world that loves to trumpet the distinction between motive and action. But Jesus obliterates the line that separates them in an all-encompassing sweep.

You see, we think: "If I wanted it, but I didn't take it, then I did a good job." But Christ seems to answer back with the question, "Why did you even want that thing in the first place?" He escalates the import of the things we tend to downplay, and he thereby causes the weightiness of the evil actions that we take seriously to become internalized—suddenly the guilt of those actions applies to us. It's an incredibly stringent position, and it is one which casts guilt upon each and every slight discrepancy. You could call it a pure, "100% uncut" ethic.

The final straw comes in the final verse of that opening chapter, when he says, "Be ye therefore perfect, as your Father in heaven is perfect."

One of my favorite contemporary Christian writers is an acclaimed University of London professor, Francis Spufford. He wrote a great book just a few years ago, called *Unapologetic*. In it, Spufford talks about this ethical conundrum into which Jesus plops us all in The Sermon on the Mount. He writes:

"Christianity makes what you mean by your behavior all-important. You could pauperize yourself, get slapped silly without fighting back, care for lepers and laugh all day long in the face of futures markets, and it still wouldn't count if you did it for the wrong reasons. Not only is Christianity insanely perfectionist in its few positive recommendations, it's also insanely perfectionist about motive. It won't accept generosity performed for the sake of self-interest as generosity. It says that unless altruism is altruism all the way down, it doesn't count as altruism at all…"

Let me just pause for a moment… how does that make you feel? It makes me feel terrible. Am I the only one tracking with him? This is a totally different approach to ethics than the one according to which most of us operate. Spufford goes on:

"[Christianity] makes frankly *impossible* demands. Instead of asking for specific actions, it offers general but lunatic principles. It thinks you should give your possessions away, refuse to defend yourself, love strangers as much as your family, behave as if there's no tomorrow. These principles do not amount to a sustainable program. They deliberately ignore the question of how they could possibly be maintained."

I don't know if you heard, but Bill Gates recently accepted a challenge from a Norwegian, named Magnus Carlson, who is the current world champion chess player. He's 23. And Bill Gates loves chess. And Bill Gates is smart. And he's a formidable fellow, one whom many people respect immensely. So they played a game on national television. And 23-year-old Magnus Carlson beat Bill Gates... in nine moves. It took 79 seconds, to be exact. Similarly, Jesus is making a move on the chessboard of ethics, one which does something that is deeply insightful.

He goes straight for the jugular, going literally to the center of our hearts, and he does so by making the religious life an inner affair. The matters of your inner world suddenly become primary. He is, in effect, declaring the seat of true religion to be the human heart, which is the real person, and the place where we all actually live most of the time, if we're being honest.

Furthermore, he does away with "ranking sins." *In this picture, there are no longer sins, just sin.* There is one river, with many tributaries, but all of it is made up of the same murky water. And, you see, that's the point. Spufford summarizes perfectly in the closing of the passage:

> "So far, it's all thrillingly impractical. But now notice the consequence of [bringing the entire human race to the point of checkmate], of having an ideal [of behavior] that is not sized for human lives: everyone fails. Really everyone..."

By taking this approach, we discover that we all stand before God on the same footing. There is no comparison to be made between you and the person sitting next to you: at least, not in God's eyes. We're talking about true equality, about a place from which we can all only utter the same prayer, which is: *"Lord, have mercy. Christ, have mercy. Lord, have mercy."*

When the Crown Prince of Austria-Hungary, Rudolf of Hapsburg, died in 1889, his funeral began with a traditional dialogue between a representative of the Royal Family and the prior of the cloister. The Master of Ceremony knocked loudly three times on the massive, closed doors of the church. The prior then answered from behind the closed door: "Who desires entry?" The answer: "Otto of Austria; once Crown Prince of Austria-Hungary; Royal Prince of Hungary and Bohemia, of Dalmatia, Croatia, Slavonia, Galicia, Lodomeria and Illyria; Grand Duke of Tuscany and Cracow; Duke of Lorraine, Salzburg, Styria, Carinthia, Carniola and the Bukowina; Grand Prince of Transylvania, Margrave of Moravia; Duke of Upper and Lower Silesia, of Modena, Parma, Piacenza, Guastalla, of Oświęcim and Zator, Teschen, Friaul, Dubrovnik and Zadar; Princely Count of Habsburg and Tyrol, of Kyburg, Gorizia and Gradisca; Prince of Trent and Brixen; Margrave of Upper and Lower Lusatia and Istria; Count of Hohenems, Feldkirch, Bregenz, Sonnenburg; Lord of Trieste, Kotor and Windic March, Grand Voivod of the Voivodeship of Serbia."

The Prior responded: "We do not know him." The Master of Ceremony then knocked again three times. Prior: "Who desires entry?"

The Royal representative answered, "Dr. Otto von Habsburg, President and honorary President of the Paneuropean Union, Member and quondam President of the European Parliament, honorary doctor of many universities, honorary citizen of many cities in Central Europe, member of numerous venerable academies and institutes, recipient of high civil and ecclesiastical honors, awards, and medals, which were given him in recognition of his decades-long struggle for the freedom of peoples for justice and right."

The Prior's response: "We do not know him." The Master of Ceremony again knocked three times. Prior: "Who desires entry?"

This time, the response was, "Otto, a mortal and sinful man."

With this, the doors to the church were flung open, with the words from the Prior: "*Then let him come in.*"

The Christian faith asserts unabashedly that all human beings stand equal before God. And it is only by His grace that we are saved. We relate to God on account of His mercy, and not on account of some system of merit and demerit, reward and punishment.

All of it points us to the cross and keeps us from getting wrapped up in details that cause us to judge our neighbors and to build ourselves up with false pretense. St. Paul writes in Romans, "*For God has bound everyone over to disobedience so that he may have mercy on them all.*"

The forgiveness of God can handle anything. And I'm not talking about all of you, plural; I'm talking about all of *you*, as an individual. The work of the Holy Spirit in a human life is all-encompassing. You stand before God completely exonerated. And thus He is just as much in the business of using your failings and shortcomings, your points of impasse and collapse, to bring about good in the world, as He is your assets and strengths. All of it is part of a sovereign tapestry. As far as God's concerned, all guilt is off the table. It will not be factored into the equation of your destiny.

Brennan Manning was a Roman Catholic monk who fell from grace when he was overcome by a terrible alcohol problem. After a period of rehabilitation, he ended up back in a monastery, where he wrote a series of wonderful books about the expansive reach of God's grace. In his story, he recounts an experience he had one day. He was feeling incredibly "hung up" about something he had done. As he prayed about it, he recounts hearing a voice, which he attributes to God.

And the voice said this: "*Forget about that stuff, and come play.*"

I close with another passage from Romans: "all have sinned and fall short of the glory of God; they are now justified by his grace as a gift, through the redemption that is in Christ Jesus." *Amen.*

THE MOST RELIABLE MARK OF THE SPIRIT (FEBRUARY 17, 2013)

"And the Spirit immediately drove him out into the wilderness." (Mark 1:12)

It is often the case that in conversation, people only imply what they really mean to be saying aloud. Language brings with it subtlety. And if you miss certain nuances, you can miss the gist of what is actually being conveyed.

I experienced an example of this not long after I moved back to the South. We had been invited by a friend to spend the 4th of July at her parents' house with some of their extended family. It turned out that the daughter's invitation had not been shared with the parents and that her mother was especially looking forward to a dinner with just the members of their family. And so it wasn't long after we had arrived that we were asked the following question by our would-be hostess: "Are the two of you going to be able to stay for dinner?" The meaning of her question was veiled, but clear. Of course, we stayed. I'm just kidding.

The Bible is no different in that it often carries with it overtones and subtext. Such is the case with the opening verse in this morning's Gospel reading, where we are told that "Jesus, full of the Holy Spirit, returned from the Jordan and was led by the Spirit into the wilderness." We find an almost identical verse in each of the three Synoptic Gospels. The version in Mark speaks a little more forthrightly: "And the Spirit immediately *drove* him out into the wilderness." Where in the Lukan account we read that Jesus "was *led* by the Spirit," the author of Mark's gospel uses a different more forceful verb to describe the movement of the Spirit, the verb *ekballei*, which can be translated in any of the following ways: to compel, to drive out, to project, to thrust, or to propel.

Reflecting upon this type of movement brings to mind another passage from Scripture, one from the third chapter of John's Gospel, where Jesus describes the work of the Holy Spirit: "The wind blows where it chooses, and you hear the sound of it, but you do not know where it comes from or where it goes. So it is with everyone who is born of the Spirit."

This morning it is fitting for us too, to think about the ways of God and the movements of the Holy Spirit. Callie asked, in her Ash Wednesday homily, "Doesn't the Spirit usually tend to shake things up?" Given the implications of this morning's lesson, and also the experience of life that many of you know all too well, I think the only fair answer to Callie's question is indeed: "Yes." The spirit of God shakes things up. It nudges, it shapes and re-shapes, it compels, it creates, it stretches, and it causes things to shift.

The great German theologian, Christoph Blumhardt, said of the Spirit:

> "Although people do sometimes have a sense of peace with God… nevertheless, in a given situation it is not so much peace with God that is the true mark of the Holy Spirit at work, but birth pangs."

So let me ask: have you ever experienced the unsettling work of God in your own life? A place where the world as you knew it was forever altered? Perhaps there was a time when your life underwent a momentous shift that reoriented your perspective dramatically. Jesus was led from the cool waters of the Jordan River out into the dry desert for a really, really difficult six-week stay. And when that time was over, he began his public ministry. People are still talking about it all these years later.

I think Grace Church experienced just such a movement quite recently, when, in 2011, our building was damaged by an earthquake. For over a year, worship could not take place in this well-loved sanctuary. You were forced to worship in Hannahan Hall, at St. Mary's Roman Catholic Church, and, among other places, at the Synagogue down the street. Grace Church experienced a clarifying and revitalizing time through being displaced and pushed out of its building.

It reminded us that the church is primarily a *people and not a place*, and that this beautiful building that is your church home should not be taken for granted. Through a huge disruption, the people of Grace were given opportunities to engage with and lean on the hospitality of other worshiping communities and neighbors from all over the peninsula. The resulting sense seems to be one of gratitude and clarified unity.

A more dramatic illustration comes from the brilliant Japanese film *Red Beard*, made in 1956. In it, we track the important work of a wise old doctor named Red Beard. He runs a hospital for the poor and seems to be tireless in his avocation. One day he receives a call about a little girl who is sick and living in an impoverished situation. When he arrives at her place of residence, a gang of thugs attempts to stop him from taking the girl to the hospital. She is valuable to them, and they don't think she'll be returned to their care if she is removed the terrible situation. The leader of the group approaches dear old Red Beard and asks him to "step outside" so that they can "discuss" the matter.

Red Beard immediately gets up and walks out into the middle of the courtyard, where he is promptly attacked by the mob. But in a series of deft and sudden movements, he beats up the entire gang, using a combination of judo, kung fu, and chiropractic know-how. He dislocates shoulders and knees and displaces Adam's apples and whatnot. Soon the ground is strewn with moaning men.

He then calls his assistant and makes the following enigmatic statement. "These men have been injured. They need help. Let us treat them before we head back to the hospital with the little girl." The two of them then proceed to treat each of the men. The wounded flinch as Red Beard approaches them... but then he *pops* their shoulders back into place. He realigns their sternums, and suddenly they find that they can breathe again. The unsettling idea is that sometimes, God may just have to beat you up in order to then heal you. I hope it is a method that would only ever be called for in the most stubborn and stuck situations. Perhaps there is a place in your own life where you feel stuck.

I wonder, too, if you are not in the midst of some kind of displacement or upheaval. Are you in the midst of adjustment, or are you perhaps just feeling caught in an "in-between phase"? If you are, I hope you will be open to the idea that your circumstances are not simply the needless pullings of a fickle world. They may, in fact, be birth pangs, brought on by the meddlesome work of the Holy Spirit in your life. *Amen.*

THE EYES OF FAITH
(FEBRUARY 19)

"...his sight was restored, and he saw everything clearly."
(Mark 8: 25)

In this evening's Gospel lesson, we are told of Christ's healing of a blind man. It is interesting to note that initially, this man was not able to see clearly. He remarks (oddly) that he sees "people walking as though they were trees." At first, his vision was seemingly not fully restored. When he saw things after Jesus had healed him, he did not see them in the same way that he remembered seeing them before his blindness had taken form. Scholars go in many different directions with this odd spiritual instance. At best, they only seem to agree that the point is quizzical.

As an aside, let me simply say that the bits of Scripture that are not smooth (like, for example, on the road to Emmaus, when "Jesus made as though he was going on ahead of them..." or the bit about Christ drawing in the dirt before dealing with the woman caught in adultery) add dimension and depth to the text. Surely we cannot easily digest even the most straightforward passages of God-breathed Scripture. And with more confusing and perplexing sections, we do well to pause and consider.

With tonight's healing of blindness, we are given much to ponder. The fact that his vision was not altogether clear and immediately intelligible to the recipient is worth thinking about. Perhaps this is because his old eyes were not so much given back to him as they were *made new.* We might say that this man was, in effect, given new eyes, eyes which perceived the world differently from the way they had perceived it before.

Now, while it is the case that some of you wear glasses, I don't think anyone here this evening is completely blind. And yet we are all hopefully drawn to church with the express purpose of wanting to see more of God in our lives and in the world around us. We may not be blind, but we are also not overly lucid. Our insights are usually limited, and our self-deception is often pronounced. We are blind, especially to ourselves.

In Romans 3, St. Paul quotes the words of the Psalmist from the 36th Psalm: "There is no esteem for God before our eyes." In the Sermon on the Mount, Jesus goes so far as to suggest that all of us even have planks in our eyes. It is a theme that runs throughout the Bible, that human beings are fraught with a limited capacity to see things clearly. Perhaps you remember just how true this was for King David, who could not understand that the priest, Nathan, was talking directly about him until it was made clear: "*You* are the man!"

But blindness is met in the Bible with God's countenance, with His refusal to allow us to remain as such. Tonight's story is not about blindness at all, in fact. It is about sight. Granted it's new sight, but sight nonetheless.

There are theologians who talk about "having a Christian worldview." And perhaps you have heard the phrase "seeing through the eyes of faith." The author of Hebrews builds upon these ideas, suggesting famously that "faith treats those things unseen as though they were seen." He is suggesting that faith is, in some crucial sense, equivalent to sight. You could call it a "sixth sense," or even a "Spidey-sense" for that matter, but it strikes me that God does indeed illuminate the way we see things. It is one of the undeniable fruits of faith.

So let me offer finally a few of the things that I think we come to see through "the eyes of faith." They are precious and give evidence for the kind of transformation that is found in the Christian life.

—The eyes of faith look for and value forgiveness. They prefer redemption to recompense. Christians are drawn to forgiveness over and against justice (or as a better means of justice). They find in forgiveness both the voice of compassion and a hope for the future.

—Along similar lines, faith pays little attention to score-keeping. It is not competitive. It receives without deserving, and it gives where there is no merit. As one person put it during a eulogy for his friend at a funeral I attended a few months ago: "he was quick to help and did so without asking questions."

—The eyes of faith are inclined to seek connection before autonomy. Most profoundly, this means that we're drawn to identify with sinners and sufferers, rather than to stand at a distance. Faith says, "There but for the grace of God go I." It is not attracted to the famed words of the Pharisee in the Temple who remarked, "Thank you for not making me like this tax collector."

—Consequently, the eyes of faith, as they say in AA, focus on the similarities instead of the differences. They look for and value universals more than particularities; they are eyes that seek out and emphasize common ground, instead of focusing on points of divergence. They refuse us the solipsistic life that is lived in a vacuum. We come to see that God's work in our own lives comes to us primarily through our relationships and involvement in the lives of others.

—Faith also sees value in things that seem to be insignificant; it sees that the mundane details of life can give birth to extremely important occurrences. In the walk of faith, each step is attended by the God who goes before us, and who knows just what we need and how best to bring it about. We can see the immense value of honesty and the emptiness of selfish material gain. It is a paradigm that regards humility to be more precious than prestige.

—Similarly, Christianity sees in service a wonderful opportunity for self-forgetfulness, which is love. Service comes before being served, and the power we are given is not for our own benefit, but instead so that we might better empower each other. Faith brings us to see that self-pity is dealt with far better when we are taken out of ourselves than when we try to puff ourselves up with puny self-congratulation.

These attributes (and endless others) are not wishy-washy or romantic abstractions about personality adjustment. They are, instead, the altered reality that is true life. It is the life that perceives the iceberg of God's permeating presence in the midst of our daily existence, one which is constantly poking its way up through our blindness, intruding in our vision that we might finally see clearly. *Amen.*

THE BIBLE IS WRONG ABOUT DOGS (FEBRUARY 24, 2013)

"Yet even the dogs eat the crumbs that fall from their maters' table." (Matthew 15:27)

This morning, the lectionary has given us readings that refer, at least in part, to animals. We read about Herod, the fox, and Jesus, the lamb, who longed to gather his children under his wings like a mother hen. And then, in this morning's Gospel reading, we find mention of another animal: the dog. The Canaanite woman says to Jesus, *"Lord, yet even the dogs eat the crumbs that fall from their masters' table."* Then Jesus answered her, *"Woman, great is your faith!"*

Given Jesus' positive assessment of her statement, it seems that if we can understand her claim about dogs, we will understand what it means to have great faith. So let us think for a moment about dogs, and what the Bible has to say about them.

Did you know that dogs are mentioned forty times in the Bible? Forty times. And, with the one exception of this morning's passage, they're talked about disparagingly in every single instance. The Bible is obviously wrong, but it speaks with one voice on the issue of canines. Here are a few examples.

This is from the Book of Judges: *"Gideon took the men down to the water. There the Lord told him, 'Separate the ones who lap the water with their tongues like a dog from those who kneel down and drink.'"* In other words, the people who reminded God of dogs were the same ones He decided were not fit to serve in His army.

Looking a little further, we find this classic verse from Proverbs: *"as a dog returns to his vomit, so a fool repeats his folly."* Yuck! Oddly enough, it's a verse which is also quoted in the New Testament in 2 Peter, implying that this anti-dog sentiment carried its way right on over into the Christian community.

And here's Isaiah, talking about Israel in a very negative tone: *"they are dogs with mighty appetites, they never have enough. They all turn to their own way. Each seeks his own gain."* Dogs here are being used to describe human appetite in all of its voracious, selfish, and undisciplined guises.

And then the New Testament is nice enough to echo all of these themes. We find Paul, in the Letter to the Philippians, using the term as an insult, referring to the Judaizers who were seeking to require circumcision of adult male converts to Christianity. He writes: *"Watch out for those dogs, those men who do evil, those mutilators of the flesh…"* If anything, the anti-dog sentiment seems to have gained momentum in the New Testament.

As a final note, in the last book of the Bible, Revelation,

we discover that *"Outside are the dogs, those who practice magic arts, the sexually immoral, the murderers, the idolaters, and everyone who loves and practices falsehood."* "Dogs" is the term describing the forsaken, the worst of humanity.

Are you wondering about what Jesus had to say about dogs, though? Perhaps he is at least silent on the issue? Nope. Jesus, who loved children when nobody wanted to give them attention, who ate with notorious sinners, who forgave adulterers, who wanted to dine with Zacchaeus, a hated criminal mob-boss type... unfortunately, he chimes in too, and in multiple places. Here's a quote from The Sermon on the Mount, the greatest sermon ever preached, where dogs get dissed: *"Do not give dogs what is sacred, do not give pearls to pigs. If you do, they will trample them under foot and then turn to tear you to pieces."* The use is undeniably derogatory.

I think we can only conclude that the Bible is wrong about dogs. Or is it?

Though we begin to see that the Biblical text has a very dark estimation of "man's best friend," more can be said. Does the Bible really hate dogs? Well, this is not quite the case. In each instance, dogs themselves are not being disregarded, but, rather, certain traits that they possess are being highlighted and applied to a description of people. Dogs are used as a portrait of relentless appetite, of myopic self-interest, and of the pursuit of the id's desires.

And it is right to speak somewhat disparagingly about these traits, is it not? They are the motives in life that produce regret, chaos, and isolation and that cause us to disregard our brothers and sisters.

But the Canaanite woman offers a completely different read on the canine species. She, instead, draws attention to their perspective on life. Dogs look to their owner for sustenance and care. They beg for their food with the humblest of expressions. Think of "puppy-dog eyes," for example. Dogs portray humility and an upward-seeking posture, a posture which, to Jesus' way of thinking, reflects "great faith" and a proper understanding of life.

Granted, it is true that Jesus was not overly preoccupied with dogs, and that fact is perhaps worth lamenting. But I hope also that this morning we can come to see why, exactly, this was the case. It was because his focus was fixed upon people.

The truth is that dogs are easier to love than people. They are far more innocent and consistent and happy-go-lucky.

But people, at their worst, can be incredibly ugly and hard to tolerate. We can be passive-aggressive and full of that most unlovely trait: self-pity. We can be harsh and forgetful and inconsistent and selfish, even though we know better.

And so it is that people need to know that God loves even them, in their unloveliness, without recrimination or conditions. His love, the love that Christ came into the world to reveal, has no strings attached. This is how the Gospel works. Like a heat-seeking missile, it targets the place in our hearts where we are most unsure of ourselves, and there, in that spot, it unleashes mercy.

The Canaanite woman knew that God had the answer to all that concerned her. It was the shape of her faith. She knew that even a single crumb of God's grace would be enough to completely satisfy her.

Can *you* see things from her perspective? Perhaps you see the One who has the mercy you need this morning, and this week. Or, even better, perhaps you can see that you have already been the recipient of many of these heavenly crumbs. Has God not blessed you with so many good things? With friends and family, and this new morning?

Let me close with the words of *The Prayer of Humble Access*, where the Canaanite woman's words live on to this day, immortalized in our liturgy so profoundly:

> "We do not presume to come to this thy table, O merciful Lord, trusting in our own righteousness, but in thy manifold and great mercies: we be not worthy, so much as to gather up the crumbs under thy table: but thou art the same Lord whose property is always to have mercy: grant us therefore, gracious Lord, so to eat the flesh of thy dear son Jesus Christ, and to drink his blood, that our sinful bodies may be made clean by his body, and our souls washed through his most precious blood, and that we may evermore dwell in him, and he in us. Amen."

SERENADING JUDGMENT
(MARCH 13, 2013)

"The Father judges no one but has given all judgment to the Son..." (John 5:22)

Listen again to these words from our Gospel lesson: "The Father judges no one but has given all judgment to the Son... he has given him authority to execute judgment."

The unavoidable word in this passage, at least to the way I hear it, is "judgment." It is a word that causes people to bristle, the kind of word that feels a bit like a speed bump or even a roadblock. It brings to mind a wagging finger, or the "tsk tsk tsk" of a school master, or (motioning with extended index finger stroking repeatedly over opposite extended index finger) "shame-shame-shame fingers." Judgment is a thing that stops us in our tracks, seemingly holding us down under the giant Platonic form of a heavenly thumb.

So we do well to think together about what it means for Jesus to be our judge. Let me offer two thoughts.

First, if Jesus is the one who has been given by God the authority to judge the world, then it is also the case that you and I have been relieved of any similar obligations. In life, in other words, it is not our job to judge. When we find ourselves doing it—looking down our noses at the people we come in contact with—we have stepped out of proper alignment with God. We have, in some sense, simultaneously tried to usurp His role and have ceased to trust Him.

Second, if Jesus is indeed our judge, then this is good news. You *want his judgment!* For his justice is full of mercy. It is fair to say that, in Christ, "the judgment of God *is forgiveness*" (Rev. J. Koch). I don't know about you, but that's the last judgment I would ever expect to be reckoned to me. It's the one verdict that I rarely offer myself.

And so it's incredibly Good News to hear that, once and for all, the final judgment of me has come down from cosmic officials, as a deep, all-encompassing, counterintuitive, refreshing word of grace. He has pled our case with three short words: "Father, forgive them."

Or to quote the words of St. John (again from this evening's lesson):

> "Very truly, I tell you, anyone who hears my word and believes him who sent me has eternal life, and does not come under judgment, but has passed from death to life. Very truly, I tell you, the hour is coming, and is now here, when the dead will hear the voice of the Son of God, and those who hear will live."

Amen.

A PERFECT THROWING ARM
(MARCH 16, 2013)

"For this reason he is the mediator of a new covenant..."
(Hebrews 9:15)

This year, in our 11 a.m. service, we have used Lent as an opportunity to revisit the services of Holy Eucharist that have shaped our Book of Common Prayer tradition. We began with the 1549 version. Then we moved on to the 1559, 1662, and 1892 expressions of that famous service. Today we enjoy the 1928 incarnation, and it is fair to say that, as far as these kinds of things go, it is a classic.

I'm a huge fan of the Book of Common Prayer—obviously (points at collar)—and this experience is one that I have looked forward to, enjoyed, and learned from. It makes me glad to see how little our communion service has changed over the last 450-plus years. But I am also greatly appreciative of the changes that have been made. It will, for example, be nice next week, when we get back to worshipping God in an intelligible tongue... and with a concern for punctuality. I digress

But since we have been looking at the sweep of our tradition, I wish to draw your attention to one of the main things that has not changed in our service. It is a line spoken by the celebrant in each and every version of the service that we have covered. And you know it, too, because you will hear it again next week in our most familiar version of the Eucharistic liturgy. It is:

> "This is my blood of the new testament, which is shed for you, and for many, for the remission of sins" (Matt 26, Mark 14, Luke 22, 1 Cor 11:25, 2 Cor 3:6).

It's a quote from the Last Supper, found in all of the Synoptic Gospels, meaning that even the most skeptical Biblical scholar would still bet money on the fact that Jesus actually said it. St. Paul quotes it in his first letter to the Corinthian church. And Lynn read beautifully a tandem expression of this same sentiment in the Letter to the Hebrews just a few minutes ago, when we heard: "For this reason he is the mediator of a new covenant, so that those who are called may receive the promised eternal inheritance, because a death has occurred that redeems them from the transgressions under the first covenant."

The words themselves are quite nice, but they would have little staying power if their meaning were not so deeply profound. They contain within them about as much theological weight as can be packed into a single verse. And so they have been remembered by Christians the world over ever since. *"This is my blood of the new testament, which is shed for you and for many, for the remission of sins."*

We are told of a "*new*" Testament, or "covenant with God," as it is sometimes called, the implication being that there was an "old" Testament that preceded it. In a loose sense the *Old* Testament refers to the Ten Commandments, but more generally it refers to the guidelines for life that were given to the Hebrews through Moses and the forebears of the people of Israel. We read about this people and the account of how they responded to God's Law in the first forty-four books of the Bible.

What we find, perhaps to our surprise (and then again, perhaps not), is that the people of God did a very poor job of adhering to the guidelines they were given. They did not act very holy, and even when they did, they did so with very little consistency or steadfastness.

Let me pause there for a moment, just to point out that, truth be told, very little has changed. The famous psychologist (and South Carolinian), B. F. Skinner, once remarked, "The only difference between men and rats is that rats learn from their mistakes." Our spiritual lives from day to day vacillate up and down like yo-yos... at least, mine does. We have checkered résumés. We can be on a roll and then suddenly fall off like the Dow Jones. Our progress can seem at times to be almost non-existent, with the love of neighbor in some cases looking more like a grim jest. Even if we take the love of our neighbor only in its narrowest, most literal, easiest meaning—well, mine don't care enough about their landscaping, or keeping quiet late at night. Perhaps your neighborhood is different.

These are some of the most pronounced themes in the Old Testament. And for the reasons I've just mentioned, insightful people like the prophet Isaiah came to see that a "new," alternative plan for human beings was needed. If only someone could cover all of the bases and do all of the heavy lifting for us, and on our behalf. They hoped for a messiah, a "mediator."

God too saw this need, so He took matters into His own hands. He sent His perfect Son into the world to be all the things for us that we have failed to be. And in so doing, the old record was set straight, and a new record was put in its place. The budget was balanced. The Apostle puts it this way in the second chapter of the Letter to the Colossians: "And when you were dead in trespasses, God made you alive together with him, when he forgave us all our trespasses, erasing the record that stood against us with its legal demands. *He set this aside, nailing it to the cross.*" That is the *New Testament*… "given for you and for many."

Perhaps this message seems a little obtuse. So let me close by using an illustration of this dynamic at play that comes from the brilliant television show *Friday Night Lights*.

In Season 4 we get to know and love a young star quarterback named Vince, who becomes the focal point of the show. In one scene toward the middle of the season, we see Vince and a buddy in local BBQ joint. An older gentleman in the checkout line approaches them. He asks Vince, "You're Vince, the quarterback for the Lions, aren't you?" to which Vince responds, "Yessir. I am."

Then the man says, "You've been doing a great job, son. You sure can throw! Your lunch is on me. You just keep it up. My name is Harvey Long, and I run Long Landscaping. If there's ever anything I can do for you, just come and see me. Thank you for playing so well, and please know that it's a pleasure to be able to buy you some of this fine barbeque."

It's a nice scene, and one which is made a little more poignant to the viewers at home because we know that Vince comes from an extremely troubled home life. His father is in prison, and his mother struggles with a severe substance abuse problem. She's been in and out of treatment centers, and we have seen Vince drop her off in the ER to detox on multiple occasions. We've also seen him drive to visit her in rehab after football practice is over. And she is practically unemployable.

But we are also aware that at this point in the show, she is making a good go of sobriety, trying to get her life back in order, in large part with the help of her son. She is in desperate need of a job.

So when Vince hears these words from Harvey Long, he gets an idea. One day he gets his mother in the car and drives to Long Landscaping. They walk into the store and find Mr. Long behind the main register. Vince approaches him and says, "Hi, Mr. Long, it's Vince, remember me? Well, this is my mother and she's interested in applying for a job."

Mr. Long says to the woman, "Oh, it's so good to meet you. Any mother of Vince's is a friend of mine." Then Vince goes outside to wait. We see him pacing up and down the sidewalk in front of the store. At one point he peers through the window where we can see the store's owner holding her application in his hands. He's looking down at it, and the mother's head is hung low.

We get to hear the man interviewing her for a moment. He says, "It looks like there are some gaps in your professional history?" She says, "Yes, well, I went through a time of personal trouble recently." And he says, "Do you have any experience with anything having to do with landscaping?"

Then the scene cuts to back outside, to Vince, as he's pacing up and down in front of the store's entrance. After a little while, his mom comes outside. She looks at Vince and says, "He gave me a job!" And then they hug. It's a lovely scene.

Vince's intercession offers a wonderful portrait of the kind of love God has for us all because of the merits of Christ. He had the résumé that you can only wish for. And because of it, God has taken us in, to be His children. Not because of our accomplishments, but because of His Son's status, Jesus' amazing performance, his perfect throwing arm. In that place we find peace with God that cannot be tarnished.

"This is my blood of the new testament, which is shed for you and for many for the remission of sins; do this, as oft as ye shall drink it, in remembrance of me." Amen.

THE WORST CHRISTIAN IN THE ROOM (MARCH 16, 2014)

"Six days before the Passover, Jesus came to Bethany, where Lazarus lived, whom Jesus had raised from the dead. Here a dinner was given in Jesus' honor. Martha served, while Lazarus was among those reclining at the table with him." (John 12:1-2)

One of the most moving portions of John's famous Gospel comes in the eleventh chapter of the book, where we learn about the time that Jesus raised a man named Lazarus from the dead after he had been in the tomb for four days.

But this morning's lesson picks up in the next chapter, after that amazing sequence of events had occurred. Here we discover that, after Jesus had accomplished this most amazing feat, he returned to spend time with the man and his family, for they were his friends. The stage is set in verse 1: *"Six days later, Jesus came to Bethany, where Lazarus lived, whom Jesus had raised from the dead."*

I wish to focus on one simple aspect of this story, which is that Jesus continued to be present in the lives of the people whose lives he impacted profoundly. The big thing had been done, new life had been bestowed, minds had been blown … and then life seemingly went on much as it had been before. Into the midst of the aftermath of the situation, Christ came again. His friendship with the people he loved endured.

This is perhaps a comforting thing to discover about the way God works in our lives. He does not meet us in the toughest moment only to then take up a distant spot in the Cosmos, removed in the way that Bette Midler famously sang about in her hit song, "From a Distance." God is not watching us from a distance. He is present by His Spirit and at work among us right now. And this will be the case tomorrow too, when you wake up on a Monday morning, facing the demands of a new week.

But even more particularly, the good news of the Gospel message comes through this morning for those of us who are feeling a little "detached" in our walk with God. Was there ever a time in your life when the importance of your faith jumped into high relief? Perhaps on the other side of a challenging series of events? Maybe something very difficult occurred, and in that trying time, your faith provided you with great comfort. Perhaps God surprised you with the way that He was able to blend together a very weird set of ingredients into something positive, something that has helped and shaped you. Or maybe you had a very disciplined Lent one year? Was there a time when you used to be more involved in the life of the church, or, if nothing else, perhaps you used to get more out of your experience of coming to church on Sundays? Certainly Lazarus's experience of Christ had this vibe. The miracle of emerging alive from a tomb had evolved into a commonplace supper with an old friend. If you can identify at all with this train of thought, then take comfort.

To presuppose that the Christian life involves a non-stop, mountain-top experience of transcendence is to take account of a few portions of Scripture while disregarding much of the narrative's whole, including passages like the one we read this morning. The truth is that spiritual maturity involves learning to trust in God when it doesn't seem like big things are afoot, coming to church when you don't feel like it, simply for the sake of something or someone else. These are the cross-shaped moments that often punctuate the faith journey.

Yesterday, I briefly left the room where my daughter was playing to grab something from another part of the house. She started to cry as I left. It was as though she didn't think I would be coming back for more fun. I think we sometimes act a little like she did with God. Of course, He's a much better parent than I am; God's the original parent.

Similarly, we often fall out of our groove with God, or, rather, into other grooves, old and self-centered ones, for example. Sometimes they're even destructive. We see an excellent example of this in the reading, where Martha is found to be doing all of the dinner prep once again, even after Jesus' famous lecture about her needing to be a little less Type A. But there she is, just weeks after the life-changing events with her brother had happened, doing it again, the same Myers-Briggs profile.

There are indeed the more fixed elements of our human

nature. Here we find that the purview of faith accounts for them, too. I remember being disappointed, for example, just after my ordination, when I discovered that I still enjoyed the taste of Ben & Jerry's ice cream. Just days after my ordination, I asked my wife if she thought that I had improved at all in wake of that big event. She affirmed what I already knew to be true with just one word: "No," she said nonchalantly. You could say that God is not surprised by recidivism, the return of our bad traits or persistence of damaging habits. Nor is He one to hold our shortcomings against us.

So we've looked just a little bit at what life as a Christian actually feels like much of the time. I remember asking my fellow Oxford seminarians in chapel one day to raise their hands if ever they felt like "the worst Christian in the room." There I was, looking at a room full of some of the most spiritual people I've ever met, and guess what, every single person in the room raised their hand.

But what about God in relationship to all of it? Well that's what I, for one, am glad to be reminded of today. He's right there, unflinchingly present, still a friend. He's come back for dinner without any hesitation.

A very funny movie called *Flirting With Disaster* came out in 1996 (I don't recommend it). It stars Ben Stiller, back when he was still hilarious, and a huge all-star cast of folks, including Alan Alda, Mary Tyler Moore, Lilly Tomlin, and many others. The film is about a grown man who decides to track down his biological parents. He was adopted as a little boy and raised in New York City.

He contacts the adoption agency that placed him as an

infant and explains what he wishes to do. They give him the name of his mother (who lives in California) and offer to pay for the cost of his travel if he will allow them to film the long-lost reunion of mother and son as a kind of documentary. To this he agrees. So the protagonist, his wife, his newborn son, the camera crew, and the head of the adoption agency (played by Tea Leoni) all fly to Orange County for the big event.

When they arrive, the scene is both tense and poignant. His mother turns out to be a Southerner, telling him that he is descended "from the family line: Beauregard," among other things. Clearly, it's going pretty well.

But then Ben Stiller knocks over the woman's enormous glass figurine collection. We, the viewers, cringe as the menagerie case shatters all over the ground. His mother runs to site of the crash and then turns to him. She tells him, *"All children break things, and all children deserve to be forgiven. You've never had that opportunity with me until now."*

A moment later the head of the adoption agency's cell phone rings. She's overheard, muttering into the phone, "you've got to be kidding me. This is unacceptable! Are you sure?... okay." and hangs up. Then she turns to Ben Stiller and says, "This is a bit awkward. There was a screw-up with the paper work back at the office. As it turns out, this woman is not your mother. *Your* mother is in Michigan."

The hostess is incensed, asks the people to leave and, as the entourage is clearing out, announces: "I'll expect you to pay for my glass menagerie collection!" It's an amusing portrait of forgiveness given, and then retracted.

The woman in *Flirting with Disaster* who turns out *not to be* Ben Stiller's biological mom is nothing like God in this regard. You see, Christ's love is never rescinded. God's clemency never finds its end. As the saying in AA goes, "When you give your lunch to a gorilla, you don't get it back." The word in theology for this is "indissoluble," and Episcopalians affirm that "the bond of salvation is indissoluble." This is because the one who has given it will not be swayed.

His grace for us is not based upon the quality of our performance. Nor is God through with us when we feel that He is not close. In fact, He's turned up for Sunday supper today. And He'll be coming around again next week too, and the week after that, and the week after that, and the week after that... *Amen.*

Thinking Positive Is Not Always a Virtue (Ash Wednesday, 2014)

"For godly grief produces repentance that leads to salvation and brings no regret..." (2 Corinthians 7: 10)

Ash Wednesday ushers in the season of Lent and marks a decisive shift in the vibe of our Church's life. To the world, looking in from the outside, we might appear to be engaging in a somewhat counterproductive avenue of thought. It might seem like a "downer," or like some church-y attempt to "keep the people down."

But we mustn't get the wrong idea about Lent. It is not designed to rain on any parades. Nor should it be thought of as a "downer." The Lenten focus on repentance underscores the importance of honesty and self-reflection, and, as such, it deepens our appreciation for the goodness of God.

Penitence is not about feeling bad. It is about honesty and self-reflection. The experience can be compared to that of looking at yourself in a mirror for the first time in a while. According to John's Gospel, such an assessment is actually a fruit of the Holy Spirit. We are given to do it for our own good, and penitence is an avenue that ultimately edifies and enriches our lives.

Consider the probing insight of our *Book of Common Prayer*. There is perhaps no more insightful passage in the whole book than the prayer of confession. I sometimes marvel at how ably it cuts to the heart of lived human experience. Maybe you remember the version we find in the service of Morning Prayer: *"We have erred and strayed from Thy ways like lost sheep. We have followed too much the devices and desires of our own hearts… We have left undone those things which we ought to have done, and we have done those things which we ought not to have done."* I have yet to meet the person who cannot identify, in some respect, with this sentiment. Who among us is a stranger to regret? Who among us has never needed to say they were sorry?

And yet we live in a world that is often quick to downplay the importance of this aspect of our inner life. Sometimes it seems like our attempts to "stay positive" have more to do with denial and avoidance of the negative than with any genuine gratitude for our many blessings, like some kind of foolish counter-balancing act which touts the line, "Pay no attention to the man behind the curtain," as the voice admonishes Dorothy in *The Wizard of Oz*. Perhaps we have lost sight of the fact that denial and defensiveness are not Christian virtues.

Hopefully we have not completely acquiesced to the *status quo* of our grooved tendencies. Lent is designed to snap us out of the unreflective, rutted life that often permeates our day-to-day trudging. It questions our ineffective methods of coping.

Of course, we are not inclined to be transparent. And we are not inclined to apologize. But we all know regret.

Perhaps our reluctance to engage with this side of life is taught to us by our culture. After all, weakness is typically understood to be a liability. Trespass is thought to be grounds for dismissal and punishment. Remember the scene in the film *Glenn Gary / Glenn Ross*, when the cut-throat Alec Baldwin tells his team of salesmen, "The person who closes the most deals wins first prize, which is a Cadillac... Second prize is: 'You're fired.'" Heaven forbid that we should ever perform badly, much less admit it!

But we do make mistakes, and we do disappoint ourselves... oddly enough, the Christian faith is predicated upon this fact. But, unlike the world, God *is* forgiving. In Him we have permission to be frail. In Christ's realm, we discover that risks are appreciated and buffered with grace.

We explore the flawed parts of our lives because in so doing, our relationship with God deepens. Our appreciation for the One "whose property it is always to have mercy" grows accordingly. Simply saying sorry to God, and then receiving His forgiveness, is a far more sane approach to life than any other I've come across.

And so we seek to build into our thinking an acknowledgment of our ongoing, daily need for grace. As Callie reminded us in today's noon-time homily, the Gospel proclaims that where there is sin, there is grace all the more. In Christ, we discover that God has plumbed the depths for us, that his loves surpasses our ability to escape it. It's the great, surprise-twist ending to the story of our failings.

Consider, finally, a rather heavy illustration of this dynamic from the Dean of the Cathedral in Springfield, Massachusetts. The Very Rev. Jim Munroe, when he was a little boy, had a fairly typical relationship with his younger sister in that they fought a lot.

One day, at the top of the main staircase in their house, Jim punched his sister in the stomach. As she hunched over, with her mouth open, in that breathless moment just before the cry kicks in, he reached for an aerosol can on the side table there and sprayed it into her open mouth. He then looked at the can, only to find out that it was DDT.

At that moment, his mother heard the screaming, ran up the stairs, saw her daughter curled up on the floor and the spray can in Jim's hand, and realized what had happened. She scooped the girl up in her arms, ran down the stairs and flagged down the first car that drove by. They headed straight for the hospital, leaving nine-year-old Jim alone in the house.

Jim recounts that he headed into his bedroom, where he sat down at the foot of his bed in shock. He was sure that he had just killed his little sister, and he knew that God was angry with him.

About twenty minutes later he heard the personification of that angry God, walking up the stairs in the familiar form of his father's footsteps. His father opened the door, looked at poor Jim, with his face all ashen white, and held out his arms invitingly. "She's okay," he said, and embraced his son as Jim ran into his arms. Needless to say, Jim's experience of grace did not cause him to revel in his bad behavior. It caused him to appreciate God all the more. Today he and his sister are best friends.

I hope that Lent, this year, will be an especially enriching time for you. May God enable it to be, for each of us, a time of honesty and a time of spiritual depth. *Amen.*

"Does Anybody Have a Real Question?" (April 7, 2013)

"But Thomas... was not with them when Jesus came."
(John 20: 24)

In this morning's famous Gospel passage, we are reminded of the experience of Thomas, the doubting disciple, who was the original "doubting Thomas." His example speaks to unbelievers and people of faith alike, for who among us is unfamiliar with doubt? So let's think about doubt, and consider what it is that happens when we waver in our faith.

Doubt, in and of itself, is essentially uncertainty. It typically takes one of two forms. The first, which is the more common of the two, is much less beneficial to a person's spiritual well-being than the other. This is because it is full of anger and self-righteousness. It does not want to be convinced otherwise. I'm referring specifically to resentment that masquerades as doubt. It claims to be doubt but has very little concern for the thing it objects to. It is usually born out of one's personal history, and it has a vehement, typically argumentative character.

One such example comes from a book called *Grace in Practice*, where the author speaks about his father:

> "My father, the son of a pastor, told me that when he was a little boy in the small town where his dad was serving, he and a friend found a drum one day and started walking up and down the street, banging it. It happened to be Good Friday, and they were German immigrants to America before the First World War. My father told me that his father whipped him with a belt as punishment, punishment for playing around on a most holy day. From that day and forever after that day, my father had no love for the church, none at all."

The passage reminds me of an encounter that occurred at a dinner party between an old Christian and a young atheist. At one point in the conversation, the young man tried to engage the old man in debate. He rattled off a list of all of the reasons why he did not believe in God. He got more and more worked up as he went along, and soon all of the rest of the guests found themselves listening in on the exchange. This young "Thomas" talked about unjust suffering, problems of verifiability; he cited Nietzsche, Feuerbach, and the problems with teleological and ontological theodicies.

He sounded very learned indeed, and also somewhat brazen, and long-winded. At the end of the diatribe, the older gentleman asked him: "If I can answer every one of your questions, and rebut every one of your arguments, will you then become a Christian?" The young man responded with a forthright "No," which prompted the older gentleman to ask the rest of the guests at the table: "Then do any of you have any *real* questions?"

The "real questions" bring us to the second kind of doubt, the kind which reaches up and out achingly. It longs to have its mind changed. This is the kind of genuine skepticism that causes us to grow and to deepen. A contemporary poet, Christian Wiman, does a beautiful job of describing it. He writes:

> "Honest doubt is different from an ironclad commitment to doubt itself. Honest doubt is painful, but its pain is active rather than passive, purifying rather than stultifying. Far beneath it, no matter how severe its drought, how thoroughly your skepticism seems to have salted the ground of your soul, faith, durable faith, is steadily taking root."

This kind of doubt is indeed a crucial component of the spiritual life. It walks with us in odd moments, lurking in the quiet that we avoid. It provokes us to rethink and to think again even the things we trust most in the world. Have you got any such apprehensions wriggling around in your soul like worms in the soil?

I remember one example from early in my ministry. I spoke with a couple who had been married for many years. The wife said of her husband, "He'll tell you he doesn't believe any of this stuff, but the moment we start to sing an old hymn, you'll see tears streaming down his face!" He was a man riddled with doubt, who, in some important sense, felt unshakably known by God.

Another important thinker described her profound experience of doubt in the following, very transparent words:

> "As for me, the silence and the emptiness is so great that I look and do not see, listen and do not hear... Where is my faith? When I try to raise my thoughts to heaven, there is such convicting emptiness that those very thoughts return like sharp knives and hurt my very soul..."

Do you know who wrote those words? It was Mother Teresa, who is now on the road to official sainthood. Perhaps they're not the kind of thoughts you would associate with a saint? But that's exactly the reason I wanted to share them with you, to look at just how integral a part of faith doubt can be.

So then, what are we to do about our doubts, as well as the doubts of others that often confront us? There are quite a few things to bear in mind.

First, arguments don't get rid of doubt. Arguments frequently cause people to become *more* entrenched in their position, especially if there is any anger involved. I made the wonderful mistake of studying philosophy in college. While my philosophy degree did prepare me well to work in the food and beverage industry, it did not cause me to mellow in my negative associations with the Christian religion. I would come home from college in much the same mind-set as the young atheist at the dinner party whom I mentioned earlier. And my father, who is an Episcopal minister and also a wise man, would listen to my ramblings without pushing back at me. I remember that I would fire away at him, and then he would say things like, "Huh, that's very interesting. I'll have to really digest that. Let me take it in and think about it." For a while, I think I even thought that I was winning our debates because he offered so little in response. But in truth, he was acting a bit like a shock absorber on a tennis racquet.

The main thing he offered me was a listening ear. It was as though he were listening not just to what I was saying, but to me, as an angry and confused young adult male. At points, he seemed genuinely to identify. Of course, he did not lose his faith in engaging with me, but I see now, in hindsight, that I was actually in the midst of my own conversion of sorts.

Picture, if you will, a long rope with a knot in it. If you pull on both ends of the rope, the knot will only constrict and get tighter. The only way to undo it is to feed rope into the knot. So it is, too, with faith. Genuine doubt is not inclined to stay put. As long as it is given space to breathe, space where God Himself can respond in His own quiet way, it almost always morphs into something that resembles conviction.

And so we, as fellow doubters, can help others who doubt by sharing what is perhaps surprising news for the skeptic: that we, too, struggle. And we can listen to and pray for those who we know are in the midst of doubting.

For, after all, as we learn from the other ten disciples in this morning's lesson, the doubter is welcome in our midst, and God alone can convince the one who needs convincing. If this account is anything to go by, it seems that He will do exactly that. Keep in mind that Thomas is not the only one who had to be convinced. Don't forget last week's reading about Mary, or what else is said this morning about the other disciples: all of them needed God to meet with them, too. And the same goes for St. Paul. None of them believed at the outset. Yet they were the ones who built Christendom.

I close with a final question: are you aware of what happened to Thomas? Scripture tells us that he came to sincerely believe in Christ's divinity, professing, "My Lord and My God!" But do you know that church history informs us that his story did not end there in that room?

Thomas went on to spread the Gospel to the ends of the earth. He traveled to India, where he started some of the first Christian churches in the region. Most of them can still be visited to this day, including his tomb, in the city of Madras, which is, I assure you, as real a place as Charleston, South Carolina. *Amen.*

Breakthrough on the Other Side of Breakdown

(Palm Sunday, 2013)

"The crowds that went ahead of him and that followed were shouting, 'Hosanna to the Son of David! Blessed is the one who comes in the name of the Lord!'" (Matthew 21:9)

Today is Palm Sunday, when we remember Christ's "triumphal entry" into Jerusalem. The scene is striking. Jesus rides into the city of Jerusalem on the back of a mule. That part of town, on the outskirts of the city, remains to this day a very poor area. When the people see him, they lay down their cloaks before him, chanting *en masse*, "Blessed is the king who comes in the name of the Lord! Peace in heaven, and glory in the highest heaven!"

Jesus' ministry has come to a major point of culmination, and he is days away from being treated so terribly by the authorities. Many of his fans believe that he is about to take over leadership of the city in the form of some kind of conquest.

Jesus embodies the hopes of the lowly and oppressed. The feeling on Palm Sunday was encouraging and full of anticipation.

But most of the thinking about Jesus that permeated the scene was misguided. Only Jesus had even a glimpse of the way that things would actually go down. By the end of that same week, and on the other side of hopes that had been building in the disciples' hearts for over three years, all of Jesus' followers would find themselves to be completely bereft. They were about to be saddled with disillusionment and disappointment, and they would soon be rendered incapable of putting all the pieces together.

Palm Sunday embodies the outcome of high hopes and great anticipation, and it is important to note that Palm Sunday's hopes play out exactly the way that most of our expectations do. Maybe you have heard the adage from AA, "An expectation is a premeditated resentment." And you know this, that things do not typically happen the way they are expected to happen. Plans butt up against life, and circumstances usually take an unexpected series of turns. In one sense, we can say that the Bible sees this side of life more clearly than we tend to. Perhaps it is from this story that the old joke takes its cue: "If you want to make God laugh, tell Him your plans."

Have you ever experienced this kind of thing yourself? Perhaps you were absolutely counting on something. I remember talking with a very bright friend of mine who applied to ten graduate schools about five years ago. He had ranked the schools in order of preference and in light of the perceived strength of their offerings. He had given months of his time to working on applications and taking entry-related exams. When the news finally came back, all of us who knew him were surprised. He had been rejected by five of the schools, waitlisted at three of them, and accepted to only two of them, his two last-choice options. My friend had been thrown for a loop. The way forward was totally unclear (and unanticipated). Major adjustments were required.

Life is full of such instances. Every day, in this sense, is full of surprises. The truth is that, just like the disciples in this morning's lesson, we do not know what life holds for us. The line that many of us have been told, that we can shape our destinies, does not always ring true. In fact, it rarely does. I remember hearing a person say, "I don't like surprises." The Christian in me wanted to say, "Well, that's too bad. Looks like you're in for a wild ride."

While perhaps this may sound like bad news, it is not. It reminds us of two crucial pieces of truth. The first is that we are not in charge of our lives. God is. In the instances where our plans are thwarted, we are reminded that we ourselves are not in charge. We do not know best, nor do we need to. Control is relinquished because it is forced from our hands. We become humble, and true faith is ignited. We comply, for a change, which is good. The truth, as it turns out, is that trusting God is a crucial component of life.

The second crucial insight also comes from our knowledge of this famous story. All of us know the ending, you see. We know the narrative that defines Holy Week, the heaviness of the Passion, and the surprise of Easter. In this sense, you and I have an advantage over the disciples that we read about.

The story does not end badly. God is not at all absent. As their hopes are being dashed, so too God's blessed work is unsheathing itself in great majesty. And fortunately, this too is always the case. God is at work; God knows what He is doing; He has not forgotten about us but is, in fact, in the process of saving us.

In a movie that came out a few years ago called *Win Win*, we see these themes at play. We learn of Paul Giamotti's character that he is a lawyer on the verge of bankruptcy. He discovers that one of his clients is a very wealthy man who is living alone at the end of his life, with no family to speak of. Paul realizes that he can become the man's legal guardian and leave him in an assisted living facility. He will, in effect, be able to collect a large monthly check without having to do anything much else for the man's care, other than an occasional visit.

But then, one day, a boy shows up at the retirement home. The man, it turns out, has a delinquent grandson that nobody knew about. And because of the sketchy legal position that Paul Giamotti has assumed, he has to take the boy into his home, essentially adopting him. It is a huge inconvenience, a total curveball, and, needless to say, the news of the boy coming to live in their home comes as an enormous shock to his wife. But it turns out to be the best thing that has ever happened to their family. As the kid comes to live with them, Paul's character is forced to admit his duplicitous legal dealings to his wife. His marriage is thrust into a place of honesty, which ultimately leads to revitalization. You could call it *the breakthrough on the other side of the breakdown*.

The movie is great because the story reflects a side of truth which most of us are inclined to avoid. And the same goes for Palm Sunday, and the trajectory of the next week in our church calendar. They are events that we remember, not just because they really happened, but because they reorient our perspective, showing us a deep-seated truth about life that we have most likely forgotten about, and need to confront.

We are not in charge. God is. And He knows what He is doing. *Amen.*

POLE-VAULTING OVER CALVARY (GOOD FRIDAY, 2014)

"And when they came to a place called Golgotha (which means Place of a Skull)…" (Matthew 27:33)

This is a solemn occasion and one which naturally lends itself to contemplation. We can take a page out of a little book that W. H. Auden published in 1970 called *A Commonplace Book*. In this excerpt, the poet places himself imaginatively in the midst of the events that we are here today to remember. He writes:

> "Just as we are all, potentially… in Jerusalem on that first Good Friday before there was an Easter…. It seems to me worthwhile asking ourselves who we should have been and what we should have been doing. None of us, I'm certain, will imagine himself as one of the Disciples, cowering in the agony of spiritual despair and physical terror. Very few of us are big wheels enough to see ourselves as Pilate, or good churchmen enough to

see ourselves as a member of the Sanhedrin. In my most optimistic mood I see myself as a Hellenized Jew from Alexandria visiting an intellectual friend. We are walking along, engaged in philosophical argument. Our path takes us past the base of Golgotha. Looking up, we see an all too familiar sight—three crosses surrounded by a jeering crowd. Frowning with prim distaste, I say, 'It's disgusting the way the mob enjoy such things. Why can't the authorities execute people humanely and in private by giving them hemlock to drink, as they did with Socrates?' Then, averting my eyes from the disagreeable spectacle, I resume our fascinating discussion about the True, the Good and the Beautiful."

He conveys the type of thoughts that we all might have had. It is certainly fair to say that the Christian religion is oddly profound in the way that it grounds itself in these seemingly horrific circumstances. And the important thing is that we don't try to pole-vault over Calvary in an attempt to get the good news of Easter too quickly.

I haven't spent much time with clay, but I remember, when I was a little boy in pottery class, learning how to join two pieces of clay together before putting them in the kiln. You probably did this yourself. What do you have to do? You have to make score marks, which are crisscrossing lacerations in the clay, in order for the two pieces to adhere well to each other. *Good Friday recounts the score marks that bind our lives to God's infinite grace.*

I was speaking recently with a woman who told me the story of a painting she inherited when she got married. Her mother-in-law presented it to her soon after their wedding, wrapped in brown paper. When she opened it, she discovered a painting of the crucifixion, very valuable, very well-done, and absolutely horrid to look upon. And so I asked her, "Where do you keep it?" She said, "I keep it wrapped in a sheet under the bed in our bedroom."

The crucifixion of Christ rips the lid off of the worst aspects of life. It exposes a fallen world, one that is deeply infected and (to quote the *Thirty-Nine Articles of Religion*) "very far gone from original righteousness." We see vehement anger, tragic confusion, mockery, and blood-thirst; we hear shouting voices, brutality, and false judgment; we encounter cowardice, abandonment, pain, extreme naiveté, darkness... and death. All of the things we are inclined to gloss over and avoid.

But the Biblical account does no such thing. The Passion receives such a lengthy and detailed treatment in the Gospels that it almost seems like the writers themselves are aware of our instincts, and they are seeking to counteract any attempts we might make to postpone or evade these dark reflections.

In a related vein, the great Japanese filmmaker Akira Kurosawa experienced a life-changing moment in 1923, when Tokyo was devastated by the great Kanto earthquake. Akira was thirteen years old at the time. In the aftermath, his older brother, Heigo, took the boy out into the streets to view the devastation. When the younger brother wanted to look away from the human corpses and animal carcasses scattered everywhere, Heigo forbade him to do so, instead encouraging Akira to face both his fears and the reality of the destruction by confronting them directly. The brilliant director later went on to cite the profound influence of this approach to life upon his filmmaking.

This also, at least on Good Friday, is the Christian approach. We pull the painting out from under the bed, at least for an hour. The Archbishop of Canterbury, Justin Welby, described a similar instance from his own life during an interview he gave last year. When asked if there were moments in his life when prayer had been "immensely significant," he recounted the following episode:

> "One occurred around the time of critical illness with our daughter who died in a car crash, and during the period after the car crash, before she died—five days. That was prayer at its rawest because it's the prayer of just, 'Oh God, help! Oh God, where are You?!' 'What's going on? You're going to do something, aren't You?'
>
> "And I suppose the deepest moment in that was finding a moment, when we were in a café actually, outside the hospital on the day Johanna died, and we were talking and praying, and we had a sense in ourselves of needing to say to God, 'Your will be done.' It's the Gethsemane prayer, 'If we must drink this cup...' We didn't use those words, but that was the essence of it.
>
> "In praying that, a sense of handing over, absolutely agonizing, and going back to the hospital and the professor of intensive care saying to us, 'She suddenly seems to be going.' (He then pauses, becoming noticeably choked up, before continuing). And that moment

in which one felt, though he didn't do it physically, the overwhelming presence of Jesus in that room... and there was a sense of handing her over. That was prayer at its most profound, in getting exactly the answer that we didn't want, most of all in all the world, and yet sensing that God was at the center of even this."

Amen.

CH-CHING! (EASTER, 2014)

"...she turned around and saw Jesus standing there, but she did not know that it was Jesus." (John 20:14)

There are three kinds of experiences to be had in life.

The first one is called disappointment. It's when you find yourself feeling let down. When you look forward to something, and then, when the actual moment arrives, it is marred by some unanticipated curveball. Expectations usually lead to disillusionment. It's a swing-and-a-miss. It's a "whiff."

Someone told me about a girl on a television show named Marnie, who walked into a room one day and announced to her friends:

> "I'm in a bad mood. You know, every morning, I wake up feeling really good, feeling like I'm ready to take on the day. Like, I don't know, I wanna say 'good morning' to strangers, the kind of stuff I usually hate. And then, without fail, something happens at the yogurt shop that really just kills my groove, and ruins my whole day."

That's the first kind of experience of life: disappointment, "the whiff."

The second, you might call satisfaction. Every once in a while, you look forward to some big day or special event, and, thanks be to God, things pull through, and it's fantastic. You order well at the restaurant. You plan meticulously perhaps, and thanks in large part to cooperative weather, everything goes according to plan. God is in His heaven and seems to be smiling down upon you. Weddings are almost always an example of this. I remember we pulled out all of the stops for my wife's 30th birthday, including a stretched limousine, a Lady Baltimore cake cut with a broadsword on the roof of a castle, and incredible food at Wild Olive on John's Island. We look back on it as one of the great successes in planning history. It went well, and we were more than satisfied.

These are the moments we spend most of our time shooting for. We laugh about their scarcity, but certainly we also experience them from time to time. The odds seem to be about 1 in 20. Like the perfect swing of the tennis racquet, when you hit the ball right in the sweet spot at the center of the strings. It's that moment when everything comes together with a neat "click," when things just "click."

The third kind of experience to be had in life is the pleasant surprise. This is the type of event we spend, by definition, almost no time thinking about. It's the moment when things take a remarkably wonderful turn for the positive. We've talked about when the good mood turns into a bad mood, and we've looked at when the good mood gets to stay a good mood. But what about when the bad mood suddenly turns into a good mood? Have you ever experienced that? Wouldn't it be crazy if you woke up at 6 a.m. on a Sunday morning and were excited to go to church? I had that crazy experience this morning. Have you ever suddenly realized that you like someone whom you thought you had made up your mind about not liking? Or have you ever discovered that you like a new food? Maybe you ordered something by mistake (like sunchokes) only discover that you've found a new favorite vegetable. (For the record, I think sunchokes are gross.)

This is the moment in life that I would call the "ch-ching moment," like on a slot machine when you pull the lever and all three rows come down in cherries: ch-ching! A friend of mine recently offered a raffle on her website, and the winner, when she found out that she had been chosen to receive the prize, made this comment on Facebook: "OMG!!! I'm soooo excited, I never win things like this!" It was a "ch-ching mo-ment." Or maybe you woke up this morning and discovered that the Easter Bunny had paid you a visit, that there was an Easter basket waiting for you in your bedroom.

This last category (which happens to be my personal fa-vorite of the three) contains the kinds of events that we are called to consider today, on Easter morning. In this morn-ing's famous Gospel lesson, we see that Mary thought she was having the first kind of experience, the ultimate "whiff." You might also notice that there's almost no mention of this second type, "the click." It's nowhere to be found in the Eas-ter story, and it just doesn't seem to be the kind of place where the Bible beds down. But the third type, the pleasant surprise—the "ch-ching"—is present by the boatload.

One of the things about the "ch-ching" category of ex-perience is that it often involves revisiting the first category, "the whiff." In Mary's case, the crowning moment of disap-pointment turns out to be her greatest moment of gratitude. She discovers that without the "whiff," she would never have noticed the "ch-ching."

Easter reminds us that God is especially in the business of redeeming the moments in life in which you have felt forsak-en. The former Archbishop of Canterbury, Robert Runcie, put it like this: *"Faith is not hoping the worst won't happen. Faith is knowing that there is no tragedy which God cannot redeem."*

Look at our lesson:

> "Mary stood weeping outside the tomb… she turned around and [suddenly discovered, to her great surprise] Jesus standing there, but she still [because she was trapped in the "whiff"] didn't realize that it was Jesus. She thought it was a gardener… And Jesus said to her, 'Why are you weeping? Whom are you looking for?' She said to him, 'Sir, if you have carried him away, tell me where you have laid the body and I will take him away.' And then Jesus said to her, 'Mary!' She turned and said to him in Hebrew, 'Rabbouni!'" [Ch-ching!!!]

These are the moments in life that God has in store for us. Where have you recently "whiffed?" And where is it that you are overly preoccupied with trying to make things "click?"

This morning, I'm here to remind you that the spiritual experience—which is the third category—is actually the most important one you can have. Even the moments when things just click are, in the light of God's grace, in fact the third type. The pleasant surprise is actually the one that frames all of our lives, whether you see it right now or not. It is God's ambush, and Easter reminds us of it. You see, *God is the best loose-ends man in the business, and you can count on Him, even when you forget to.*

Happy Easter! *Amen.*

THE MOST IMPORTANT MEAL OF THE DAY (APRIL 14, 2013)

"'Come and have breakfast.'" (John 21:12)

This morning's Gospel lesson familiarizes us with the surprising ways of God. We see that Jesus appeared to his disciples back in Galilee, where their journey together had begun three years earlier. Clearly these men were trying their best to return to the life they had known before Jesus had come on the scene. But God is not the type to abandon people when morale is low. And so Jesus comes to them, right when they least expect it, and at the point when they have decided that God's work in their midst has come to an end.

Christ calls to the men in their boats after a long night of uneventful fishing. He tells them to cast their nets to the other side of the boat, and immediately, the nets are filled to the point of breaking. It's as though God has chosen to reward them.

And then he calls them with the profoundly conciliatory words, "Come and have breakfast." (I was joking with the

Rector before the service that if these words were translated into contemporary New York City lingo, they would read, "Come have brunch.") We see, in this gesture, an unanticipated display of kinship, continuity, and goodwill.

And, if that's not enough, we then hear the way Jesus addresses Peter. He reinstates Peter as the leader of his church, as his successor. The calling has not been revoked due to an accumulation of demerits. Peter has a hard time with this and is not quite able to believe that Jesus would be so quick to put aside the betrayal that marked their previous final encounter. But Christ is undeterred. And so he tells Peter three times, once for each denial, to "Feed my lambs."

In each of these instances with the disciples, Jesus' words are, without exception, words of grace. A friend of mine, the Reverend Jacob Smith, recently shared a little reflection about these events with me. He makes an obvious, but helpful, point. These are his words:

> "I have wondered what I would have done had I been Jesus coming out of the tomb. I probably would have come back for vengeance: 'Ladies, tell those disciples, my so-called friends, I am bringing the heat; after I deal with Rome, and those self-righteous Pharisees, I am coming to put the hammer down' ...Praise God, I am not Jesus, and there is no hammer."

Jacob's words are helpful because they draw out just how special the grace of God really is. It is foreign to our typical way of thinking. And so we do well to emphasize these events this morning. Where Christ is present, there is grace enough for the entire world. As our prayer book reminds us: it is God's "property *always* to have mercy." Grace is like a wide river that runs parallel alongside the tiny tributary of our instincts, just over the shore from our vantage point, if only we could see it.

Have you ever experienced one of these unanticipated moments of grace in your own life? One such example from my own life occurred after my second date with my wife, Deirdre. You see, after many push-ups and careful strategizing, I had managed to get her to go out with me a second time.

The restaurant, a very hip spot in the East Village, had been carefully chosen. All seemed to be going very well until the waitress brought me the check. A few moments after I gave her my card, she returned and handed it back to me, informing us, "Your card has been declined." Talk about a red flag! I was mortified, and Deirdre ended up paying for our meal. I knew I had blown it.

But the next day she called me to tell me that she had "had a great time last night." She thanked me for taking her out, thereby offering me the opportunity to ask her out on a completely undeserved *third* date. The rest is history.

An even more profound illustration of grace comes from a short story called "Thank You, Ma'am" by the great African-American writer, Langston Hughes, in which we encounter the words of Mrs. Luella Bates Washington Jones, as she talks with a boy she caught stealing her purse:

"If I turn you loose, will you run?" asked the woman.

"Yes'm," said the boy.

"Then I won't turn you loose," said the woman [to

the young thief]. She did not release him. [Instead, she takes him to her home, and tells him to wash his face.]

"You gonna take me to jail?" asked the boy, bending over the sink.

"Not with that face, I wouldn't take you nowhere," said the woman. "Here I am trying to get home to cook me a bite to eat and you snatch my pocketbook! Maybe you ain't been to your supper either, late as it be. Have you?"

"There's nobody home at my house," said the boy.

"Then we'll eat," said the woman.

[After supper she brings out dessert.] Then she cut him a half of her ten-cent cake.

"Eat some more, son," she said.

"Come and have breakfast." "Feed my sheep." *Amen.*

I Don't Think You Understand How This Gift Certificate Works

(May 5, 2013)

"My peace I give to you. I do not give to you as the world gives." (John 14:27)

At the close of each of our services, the celebrant typically offers a word of blessing. We usually say, "The peace of God, which passes all understanding, keep your hearts and minds in the knowledge and love of God..." You've heard it many times before.

This morning's Gospel lesson brings us a verse that relates directly to those words. Jesus tells his followers, "Peace I leave with you; my peace I give to you. I do not give to you as the world gives." He offers peace to the world, but suggests that his peace is not *of* the world, which means that it "passes understanding," that it parts ways with our typical train of thought.

In order to better appreciate the peace of God that is found in Christ, we do well to consider the (so-called) "peace" that the world *does* offer. What do typical promises of peace look like? I remember growing up in a house where I constantly seemed to be at war with my mother about whether or not I had written certain thank-you notes. In her mind, we would have peace in our house only after the overdue notes had been sent off in the post. The debt of gratitude to another would no longer remain outstanding. And with her peace of mind would come a fresh and peaceful period between the two of us.

But this approach to peace brought with it a scenario that I always dreaded, that of "the next thank-you note." They never seemed to be finished. The moment that one had been written, the need for the writing of another one would present itself. And so it began to seem like the peace promised was actually a fiction, or a short-lived event, punctuated primarily by a lack of peace.

As an adult I've come to see much of life's peace through the same lens. The dishes are clean, but the machine needs to be emptied. And then it quickly fills itself back up and the cycle repeats itself. The moments when all of the dishes are clean and put away are temporary in the extreme. It seems to me that most of the avenues to peace which we pursue operate similarly. We get hungry, and then we fill up, but the sated feeling does not last, no matter how much we eat. We buy the things we want, only to find that we soon want more. The end-point in the routine never seems to surface. Peace of this kind is fleeting, even illusory. The Rolling Stones put their finger on it when they sang, "I can't get no satisfaction."

One might suggest that the search for a-peace-that-can-be-earned is a futile affair. Of course, we should not stop saying thank-you, and we should not stop eating or doing the dishes, but we can recognize that these necessities will never provide us with a lasting sense of peace. Life just doesn't work that way.

But the Gospel message does. It is good news for this exact reason. You see, unlike the peace of the world, the peace of God lasts. The forgiveness of God is not a bait-and-switch trap. It does not expire. When Jesus uttered those fateful words on the cross, "It is finished," he meant what he said. The heavenly parking meter is not ticking.

Imagine, if you will, a cup of coffee that never needs topping up. Jesus described just such a scenario when he spoke with the woman at the well. He saw the problem I've been describing, and he offered an alternative solution. Here are his words: "Everyone who drinks of this water will be thirsty again, but those who drink of the water that I will give them will never be thirsty" (John 4:13-14).

Of course, this is a hard thing to wrap our heads around. It is a foreign commodity, a kind of currency that does not suffer from inflation.

A few years ago, just before Christmas, I received a very generous gift certificate to a local, high-end department store. The man who gave it to me was a member of my congregation and also the owner of the store.

About two weeks after I received it, I went into his store to make use of it. He met me at the entrance. I proceeded to select a lovely sports coat, one which I could wear in both professional and social settings, plus a nice dress shirt and some fancy loafers. I made sure to look at each of the price tags (on the sly) as he showed me different items that he thought would suit me well. In my head, I spent much of the time doing some calculations. My plan was to overshoot the gift certificate enough to be able to then put a bit of cash back into the store's register, thereby showing my gratitude for the generosity I had been shown and also displaying my support for his shop.

When I got to the register, he proceeded to tally up the total. I put my wallet on the counter and got my card out of my wallet. But as he turned to face me, he placed the gift-certificate down in front of me, and said, "It looks like you've only spent a little more than half of your credit with us." I was mortified. In that moment I realized that he had only been charging me half of the ticket price. It meant that I was still in his debt, and the feeling accompanying this realization was quite uncomfortable.

I knew what had to be done and explained the entire situation to Deirdre upon my return home. She agreed to accompany me back to the store in a few weeks' time, where she would "help" me spend the rest of the credit by finding some new clothes for herself. We agreed that we would spend well over the remaining amount, in a further attempt to show our appreciation.

So we did just that. After a little shopping, we approached the counter as a unified front, and with a veritable armload of wears we wished to acquire. I handed our friend the gift certificate. He took the gift certificate in hand and then began entering the purchases into the register, bagging them up one by one as he went along.

Finally, when the bags were full, and everything had been rung up, he turned to us with a look of seeming amazement on his face. "You're not going to believe this," He said, "but I've rung everything up, and the total comes to exactly *zero*." We were horrified, and protested a bit. "That can't be right. The total should be well above what was left of our store credit, etc..."

Then he got serious, and he said, "I don't think you understand how this gift certificate works. *No matter what you throw at it, the total will always continue to come up reading zero*." It was the first moment we understood the nature of the situation, which, for us, had to be spelled out. In our attempts to buy our way out of the debt, we had completely missed out on seeing the value of the credit, of the gift, which this generous man took such pleasure in bestowing upon us. There were no words. And are you wondering if he gave me another comparable gift certificate again, for Christmas of the following year?

The work of the cross, for you and for me, carries with it the inescapable reckoning of God's peace with the world, which is a trustworthy, unwavering, and everlasting promise to the world. Let us close with the blessing:

> "And may the peace of God, which passes all understanding, keep your hearts and minds in the knowledge and love of God, and of his Son, Jesus Christ our Lord, be among you and remain with you always. Amen."

FOR HIS EYES ONLY
(MAY 8, 2013)

He replied, "It is not for you to know the times or periods that the Father has set by his own authority. But you will receive power when the Holy Spirit has come upon you; and you will be my witnesses in Jerusalem, in all Judea and Samaria, and to the ends of the earth."
(Acts 1:7-8)

I see Jesus doing two distinct things in these verses. First, he takes something that should be rather straightforward, and he turns it into something enigmatic. He turns something clear into something confusing. Then, after doing this, he makes the exact opposite move, turning something that seems hard to grasp into a thing that sounds fairly matter of fact. In other words, he makes something opaque into a thing that is clear.

His disciples ask him when he will "restore the kingdom to Israel." It seems to them that Jesus should be able to give them a timeline, or even a date. Their question is, in effect, when will such and such happen? But Jesus' answer is anything but an answer. He says, "It is not for you to know the times or periods that the Father has set by his own authority." It's the last thing they want to hear. And yet it's a classic position, the kind the Bible famously takes at so many points, especially at the times when we try to pin God down. We are told that we do not get to know.

I see in this an implicit idea, which is that God will never give us so much information about our life that we will be able to get the impression that we are in control. In fact, to the extent that we try to get control, He actually thwarts our efforts. Perhaps we shouldn't be asking these kinds of questions.

So let me ask you, what is it that you wish to know about your future? It is my hunch that God will leave you in the dark about those exact matters, at least until after they have come to pass or have been divinely circumvented.

The second move that Jesus makes meets the disciples on the other end of their thwarted attempt to control him. He reminds them that the Holy Spirit will "come upon them," and that they will be his witnesses to the ends of the earth. It's as though he's telling them that, while they're not able to even begin to control his movements, that he will nonetheless remain committed to them in the midst of their confusion. The implication is that God's presence in our lives is a very real thing. God, who seems far off, is actually near. The Spirit is at work, even in the details, weaving them together like an eternal loom.

I experienced a version of these two trains of thought when my wife and I first moved to Charleston. At the time, I was working at Church of the Holy Cross on Sullivan's Island.

One weekend, my wife and I went antiquing in Walter-boro. We were looking for a new coffee table. Soon after entering a small shop, my wife discovered a beautiful, old, wrought-iron flower box, which, she quickly became convinced, would make a perfect coffee table if we just turned it on its side and got a piece of glass cut for the top. The owner, a very nice lady, asked us where we were from, and we told her, "Charleston." She mentioned that she had grown up in Charleston, on Sullivan's Island. My wife commented that I, her husband, currently worked on Sullivan's Island. The lady mentioned briefly that her father had served as an Episcopal priest at the little church there, a place called Holy Cross. Flabbergasted, my wife responded, "My husband is one of the ministers at that church!" Everyone got the chills.

Clearly God wanted us to have this coffee table, and through a seemingly random, far-fetched series of events, He had made it obvious that our entire day had been part of a much bigger plan. We returned home, with our new coffee table component in tow, excited to finally get it into the home where it had been destined to serve.

An hour later, we were home, carrying the flower box through the front door and into the living room. We sat it down in the middle of the room, up-ended so that we could see what it would look like... It was not right at all. It looked terrible.

God is certainly in our midst, but what exactly He is doing in our lives at a particular moment is rarely a thing that can be easily perceived. *Amen.*

THE SHAPE OF (CHRISTIAN) LOVE
(MAY 12, 2013)

"Do not harm yourself, for we are all here." (Acts 16:28)

The Christian religion brings with it many claims about God and about life. Perhaps the most basic tenet we espouse about life has to do with the emphasis we place upon the importance of love. Along these lines, it should be noted that Christian love is not merely a trite abstraction or reiteration of the Beatles' song "All You Need Is Love," though I for one wholeheartedly sympathize with the sentiment of that classic tune. While it is certainly right to suggest that we need more love and to encourage and foster more rather than less of it at all costs, it is not hard to see that such exhortations seem to be limited in their concrete impact. This is because we are bombarded on a daily basis by the absence of love.

Unfortunately, the 60s did not change this fact. The absence of love continues to throb in and around us like a migraine headache. There's never enough of it. And it rarely seems to be present in the places and times when it is most needed. While some people might suggest that love is an easy and accessible commodity, I personally am not convinced. To my way of thinking, love is hard and elusive, even rare. When it makes an appearance, it stands out in a most pronounced and radical way.

This is the case in this morning's reading from Acts, where we learn about the imprisonment of Paul and Silas. It's one of my favorite stories in the Bible, so allow me to retell a bit of it.

We are told that, by way of healing a possessed woman, Paul and Silas got in between some men and their golden goose. You see, after their encounter with her, she could no longer tell the future. Think: reformed palm reader tries to peace out on the mafia. These men, in turn, stirred up a crowd and had Paul and Silas arrested and tried in a kangaroo court of sorts, where the two of them were convicted on trumped-up charges. After being beaten severely, the two men were thrown in prison. We are told too that the jailer was commanded to "guard them carefully."

One cannot help but feel for Paul and Silas. To call their experience "a bad day" would be a serious understatement. It's at this point that we encounter the first of many surprising twists in the narrative.

Luke tells us in the next verse: "[at] about midnight Paul and Silas were praying and singing hymns to God, and the other prisoners were listening to them." What a striking, otherworldly thing this is to imagine! They were thanking God for their difficulties. And we are told that this display made a tremendous impression upon the other prisoners, which is not all that surprising if you think about it. When suddenly God used an earthquake to cause their chains to fall away, and to open the doors of each of the cells in this county lock-up, the rest of the prisoners were so blown away that they decided to take their cues from Paul and Silas.

Now this all happened in the middle of the night, and there was no electricity. You can imagine the jailer's horror when he saw the door to the jail's entrance gaping open. He could only have assumed one thing, that all of the convicts had escaped. Can you imagine the trouble that a prison warden would be in if all the inmates escaped under his watch? Surely he felt at that moment that his life was over.

But that's exactly when he heard a voice calling to him through the open door, from within the darkness. It was Paul, and he said, "Do not harm yourself, friend. You do not need to worry, we are all still here." Can you picture the jailer's great surprise? Not a single man had escaped! And why? Because they didn't want anyone to get in trouble on their account. The prisoners were thinking about the well-being of the guard, even at a moment when it seemed like God Himself was facilitating their escape.

Now that is a portrait of Christian love. All of the ingredients are in place. We see sacrifice for the sake of another, deep concern for others; it is a complete rewriting of the types of things that normally take place. Self-interest is seemingly nowhere to be found.

This is grace, the great and miraculous surprise that is found in God's goodwill. When it catches you in its sight, it melts your heart and causes scales to fall from your eyes. It inspires, and it creates in its recipient an unlikely advocate.

As St. John puts it, "We love, because he first loved us."

We are told that the jailer, when he realized what had happened, "rushed in and fell trembling before Paul and Silas." In that instant, he became both their devoted friend and a famous proponent of the Christian message. In the unfolding of this story, you and I are most likely inclined to identify with Paul and Silas... but not the jailer. And that's our mistake. Fortunately it is not God's.

Now much can be said about this profound dynamic and its implications. It makes me think, for example, of that song by Huey Lewis and the News: "that's the power of love." But I want to offer only two brief thoughts. The first is that the Christian faith suggests that meaning in life comes from living for the sake of others. There is no fulfillment to be found in self-fulfillment. By contrast, it is self-emptying that produces happiness and purpose. Martin Luther put it like this: "A Christian lives not in himself, but in Christ and in his neighbor." This is the shape of love.

Second, I'd be remiss on Mother's Day if I didn't point out that there is no better expression of it to be found on earth, than the one we find in the love that is shown to us by our mothers. They literally give up their own bodies to make our lives possible. They spend huge amounts of time and energy working for the benefit of their families. Can you think of a less deserved, and therefore more moving, example of abiding love?

I can only think of one, and that is the love of God that is found in Christ. His was a love that gave up everything it possessed, even to the point of death, for our sake, so that we might live. May God fill our hearts with this love. *Amen.*

IN-BETWEEN (MAY 18, 2014)

"'Lord, we do not know where you are going. How can we know the way?'" (John 14:5)

Today's five-dollar word is "liminal." Do you know the word liminal? It's an adjective, defined as:

1. of or relating to a transitional or initial stage of a process.

2. occupying a position at, or on both sides of, a boundary or threshold.

It's often used in the study of anthropology and psychology to describe ceremonial moments that demarcate points of transition. So, in a tribal culture, if one is about to perform or be a part of some kind of ritual that marks growth from boyhood into manhood, that is a "liminal phase." Familiar examples include things like Bat Mitzvahs, graduation from college, and weddings. In psychology, if you are occupying a position that places you on both sides of a thing or in the midst of crossing a boundary or a threshold, then you are in a "liminal stage."

It's basically a fancy word for "in-between." I've been thinking about liminal moments this week for obvious reasons. Summer is now here, but we are on the front end of it. Everyone is getting out on the water again in some fashion. Vacations are imminent. People have headed to the mountains (or various places). The feeling in town has noticeably shifted along seasonal lines.

Similarly, graduations are occurring all around us. This past Friday we ushered The Little School, Class of '14, into elementary school. And last Saturday we had commencements for both the College of Charleston and The Citadel. Plus, the news is rife right now with different noteworthy commencement addresses and all of the hubbub surrounding graduations.

But on top of that, we had a funeral here this past week. Funerals definitely mark a point of transition. And then we had a Newcomers' Welcome event this past Thursday up in the Meadowcroft Room. Thirty-five new people have just joined Grace Church. For them, this is a liminal time. I met a five-week-old baby named Camden, our newest member. Life is his new phase. We're baptizing a child at 11:00, a little boy, Fuller. Liminal in the extreme.

It strikes me that life is full of these types of experiences, of transitions, of next phases, and of "in-between-ness." The Greek philosopher, Heraclitus, put it like this: "You can't stick your foot in the same river twice."

We are all engaged with a future that is barreling toward us. Its unfolding is imminent.

With that said, there are two things I wish to say about

the future this morning, about the events that will soon come to pass.

First, if you think you know what is going to happen, you don't, and you're probably going to be disappointed. There are a few reasons for this (and I'm not trying to be a downer, and I'm also not telling you something you don't already know).

But life in this fallen world is full of curveballs. What's it called again—Murphy's Law—you've heard of that? It's not that bad things will happen, but that whatever *can* happen *will* happen. And we don't know all of the things that can happen on the front end, do we? The result is that things usually go a different way than we expect them to go. Accurate predictions are as rare as hen teeth. I remember a few months ago when everybody's college basketball bracket was blown out of the water after Mercer beat Duke. Do you remember that? Life does not bend to speculation all that well.

The problem is not so much that life works this way as it is that even though we *know* it works this way, we still expect it not to. The result is usually some form of upset apple cart. There's a saying in AA, "an expectation is a pre-meditated resentment." Put in more spiritual terms, we might posit: God's way is probably not *your* way. Indeed, it is hard (going on impossible) to pin God down.

Given this assessment, I empathize with Thomas's words to Jesus from this morning's Gospel lesson. They're a no-brainer. He said, *"Lord, we do not know where you are going. How can we know the way?"*

God knows that life is going to require improvisation from you. In the Bible, that kind of improvisation is often

141

called "faith." It's the place where life's moguls meet your unanticipated adjustment. (The films *It's A Wonderful Life*, *Miami Vice*, and *Finding Nemo* offer great portraits of this kind of holy scrambling, by the way.)

The second thing I want to say is that it is in that place— in reality—that God is always to be found. Christ's answer is as straightforward as we would hope it to be. He said to Thomas, "*I* am the way."

Perhaps you have just been hit by a curveball. The good news is that something new, which is indeed something of God, is going to take the place of whatever it is that you thought was going to happen. Huge portions of Scripture attest to this type of spiritual experience. The psalmist, for example, wrote 150 poems to that effect. In the place of disappointment, we discover that life is not over, and that God is not through with His good works.

In my own life, I've never been happier than I was six months after the breakup that I thought would kill me. And I've never been more fulfilled professionally than I was just after the time when I lost my job due to events that I could not control.

If you want to take something home from this sermon, go home and put on Peter Frampton's famous live album from 1975, and listen to "Show Me the Way." Or, if you're really cool, put on your cassette tape of Dinosaur Jr.'s cover of that song from 1987.

He "is the way." What a relief! *Amen.*

A Quiet Little Pact with Despair (Pentecost, 2013)

"When you send forth your spirit... you renew the face of the ground." (Psalm 104:30)

Today is Pentecost, when we remember and celebrate the coming of the Holy Spirit, who is the third person of the Trinity and the active spiritual presence of God in our midst.

The topic brings to mind a little story of something that happened to me in seminary. One day, when I was running late for a lecture, I slipped into the classroom through a side door and took a spot on the other side of the room from where I usually sat. As the professor called my name during roll call, he said, "John Zahl?" and looked up toward the side of the room where I was normally to be found. I answered from my new spot on the other side of the room, "present," which prompted the teacher to turn his head to see me. He then remarked, "Oh, you've changed seats. The Holy Spirit must be at work in your life."

His point, at least in part, was that people do not typically change seats, and that when they do, something spiritual is the reason for such an unexpected shift. It is an idea that relates directly to our thinking about Pentecost, I think.

By way of explanation, let's consider the work of the Holy Spirit within the context of a single verse from the day's Psalm. The Psalmist writes of God in these words: "when you send forth your spirit... you renew the face of the ground." He speaks specifically of renewal, which is a word worth pondering. What do you think of when you hear the word "renewal?"

It is a word that means "making something new again." The image we are given is that of ground being renewed, of spring coming after winter, or of rain coming after drought. It is about dead and unproductive land becoming fertile and lush once again. The metaphor is not subtle, and its range of application is wide: it can relate to any part of our lives or community that feels lifeless, or stuck in a rut. Who doesn't want their life to be creative and lush with life instead of dry and stuck?

So with that theme in mind, let me ask a question on the front end of this sermon: Do you really believe that the Spirit of God can and will renew the fallow ground in your life, that there really is renewal to be had in the part of your existence that seems hopeless or unfulfilled? Or, almost without realizing it, have you made a quiet little pact with despair? (Let the question sit with you.) Has some part of you accepted that repetitions are the fact of the matter, that they cannot and will not ever change? Have you put a brave face on this conclusion by calling it "realism," when really what you are is resigned to despair, and lacking in hope?

Consider a few examples of despair. Despair that a child will never find her way in the world. Or despair about the situation with your spouse, that you will never really be happy in your marriage. Or we might be talking about your professional life. As a minister, it hasn't taken me long to learn that most people are quite unhappy in their work. Or perhaps we're talking about despair over the state of the Church, over the perception that our culture has lost its appreciation for the value of faith.

In each of these situations, there is the temptation to think of oneself as some kind of a tragic hero, quietly fighting a long defeat in the face of overwhelming odds. Have you become, to your way of thinking, a bit of a martyr in some pronounced area of your day-to-day life? This too is a pact with despair.

In these places, what we need is renewal. And it is important to note that as Christians (especially on the day of Pentecost), we believe that renewal is always a possibility, an outcome that is just as viable as any of the current stagnancy that you are facing. We believe that the most impenetrable situation is not necessarily set in stone. Renewal is possible.

But where is it to be found?

Allow me to make two observations. First, when God brings renewal, He does so by engaging with us in our deep desires and feelings. When God's Spirit creates renewal, it does so through harnessing our real energies, through attraction, and not through force. If you seek lasting renewal, look to your real desires, the durable ones, the places that restore your energy instead of sucking it dry. God's spirit does not work through heavy-handedness or ideology or force of will; it works through joy and desire and love. In this sense, renewal is usually experienced as a freedom from some kind of bondage.

The second point is the one that I am more hesitant to talk about, but it is unavoidable. It is that the path to renewal usually leads first through suffering and thwartedness and defeat. The shipwreck of our plans and dreams for ourselves is typically the place where new life begins.

This is what the former Archbishop of Canterbury, Rowan Williams, refers to as the "cruciform" shape of the Christian life. The Christian Church was founded on Calvary, at the foot of the Cross, and that is both the once-for-all-time fact and foundation of the religion, *and* it is also the pattern God's Spirit continues to employ in its renewing work.

The Spirit of God is not a magic spell, nor is it an escape hatch. It is a deep spiritual reality that engages, often directly, with the places where our ground is most fallow. It brings with it an element of intervention. Renewal comes from the ashes. I have seen this over and over again, in the lives of fellow believers and also in my own life. Along these lines, I feel sure that the current vibrancy and unity that we are experiencing as a church here at Grace, is directly connected to the fact that less than two years ago, our congregation was displaced when our building was damaged in an earthquake. Perhaps you've experienced your own personal version of an earthquake.

The first aspect of the experience of renewal usually has to do with giving voice to frustration. Have you discussed the stagnancy you feel with God and with an outside party, such as a clergy person, or a therapist (and I'm not talking about your spouse)? I encourage you to express your need for renewal, rather than keeping those disappointments quietly at bay in the wings of your consciousness. The Spirit of God draws the darkness into the light.

What I'm really saying is that *the key to renewal is often the experience of its opposite.* As the Sufi poet Rumi puts it, "the light can only enter into the wound."

I was struck by these themes during a conversation I recently had in New York City with an art historian. I was trying to engage him about his area of expertise, so I asked him who his current favorite artists are. Rather than give me a list of names, he told me that he has a particular area of interest. He looks for artists who have been incredibly successful until, for some reason or another, the market has lost interest in their work, artists who have experienced collapse on the other side of accolade. It is his theory that great artists create their greatest works only after they have experienced some form of a collapse or defeat. Did you know, for example, that Rembrandt suffered terrible personal and financial trouble during the end of his life? His last painting, coincidentally or not, is one of the great works of European art, *The Return of the Prodigal Son.* I'm sure you've seen it. It makes the point perfectly.

Finally, let me leave you with a new question: is it now the time, at last, to give up on your pact with despair? Is it time to trust again in the reality of the life-giving Spirit of God? Is it time today, once again, to have hope and to believe once more in renewal? Let us pray:

Come Holy Spirit, and bring new life.
Create a way forward where we are blocked.
Renew love and passion where they have faded.
Harness our desires and make your Kingdom lovely
       in our sight.
Break off the repetitions and lead us down new and
       unexpected paths.
Meet us where we suffer and are unfulfilled.
Inspire us as we build and work and create.
Give us our food in due season, and renew the face
       of the ground. *Amen.*

THE RASHOMON EFFECT
(PENTECOST, 2014)

"All were amazed and perplexed, saying to one another, 'What does this mean?'" (Acts 2:12)

It's appropriate to baptize two little babies on the same morning in our church calendar when we remember the Holy Spirit's arrival on Pentecost, when the Spirit of God filled the room in which the disciples were sitting like a rushing wind and like flames of fire above their heads, after which the disciples began speaking about the Lord (publicly) in a way that oddly proved to be intelligible to people of every nation and region of the world as it was then known.

In thinking about that day 2000 years ago, 50 days after Easter, one might say it's as though God issued a report about Himself which was to be shared with the entire world. It was news about Christ, news so moving that it propelled these early Christians to proclaim it aloud. In response, we are told that more than three thousand people in the crowd asked to be baptized on that very day. This Good News has been issuing forth into the world ever since.

Now let me switch gears for a second. Have you ever heard of something called "The Rashomon Effect?" The Rashomon Effect is a term often used in journalism to describe *contradictory interpretations of the same event by different people*. The phrase comes from a great Japanese movie, *Rashomon (1950)*, in which four witnesses give different accounts of the same crime. The Rashomon Effect simply refers to the presence of competing narratives.

We see a bit of this at play in the story of Pentecost found in this morning's lesson from Acts. We're told that when the disciples were moved to address everyone in all of those various tongues, many of the witnesses were "amazed and perplexed, saying to one another, 'What does this mean?'" Others made fun of them, and said, "'They're drunk.'" At that point, Peter stood up with the Eleven, raised his voice, and addressed the crowd, saying, "These people are not drunk, as some of you suppose. It's only nine in the morning! No, this event was anticipated in the Hebrew Scriptures by the prophet Joel: 'God says, I will pour out My Spirit on all people.'" (Do you see it?! The Rashomon Effect, competing interpretations of the same event...)

One of my favorite modern theologians is a man named Alistair McGrath. There was a joke in seminary at Oxford that it was nearly impossible to find a book in our library that had not been written by him. His most recent two books are about C. S. Lewis. In an interview last week, Dr. McGrath was asked about this theme of competing narratives in Lewis's classic collection of stories about Narnia. Here is his answer:

"When the four children enter Narnia in *The Lion, the Witch and the Wardrobe*, they are told different stories about the kingdom. One story they hear tells them that the White Witch is the real ruler of Narnia. It is her kingdom, and she is entitled to rule it. But they also hear another story—that Narnia is the realm of the noble lion Aslan, and the witch is a usurper. When Aslan returns, he will overthrow her and restore the kingdom. Both stories can't be true! Gradually, the children realize that the second story is right. Lewis wants us to realize that we live in a world shaped by stories. Some are told to deceive—for example, the story that this world is an accident, and that we have no meaning. Lewis wants us to search for, and discover, the true story that makes sense of the world and our lives—the Christian story."

And this is ultimately what Pentecost is about. We are here this morning to reaffirm the Christian story in the midst of life in a world which is riddled with competing narratives.

In the news yesterday, I read two different headlines almost back-to-back. The first: *Thirteen Injured after South Carolina Deck Collapses During Photo Op.* I was fascinated and read on:

"A deck at an oceanfront inn on Pawleys Island, near tourist hotspot Myrtle Beach in South Carolina, collapsed while over twenty-five people attempted to take a selfie in front of a rainbow over the ocean. Over a dozen people were injured…"

The subtext of the article is a tad cynical. It is one that perhaps views suffering to be life's ironic and darkly humorous punch line. The next article contained the headline, *Teen Begins 40-mile Walk with Younger Brother on His Back*. It read:

> "Hunter Gandee, a fourteen-year-old from Michigan, has begun a 40-mile trek while carrying his seven-year-old, 50-lb brother on his back. Braden Gandee, who is a first grader, has cerebral palsy and typically uses braces, a walker, or a power chair to get around. The walk aims to raise awareness for the condition... The family isn't asking for donations for the walk, but rather asks that anyone interested in helping send donations to the University of Michigan Cerebral Palsy Research Program."

Do you sense the difference in outlook? The second is one which resembles the Christian understanding of life.

These two sweet children, our baptismal recipients, are just beginning their lives in this world, and while their stories will certainly not be devoid of difficulty as they butt up against the realities of life, there is a bigger story at play, one that subsumes the hardships of life by breaking into ours with the enduring and transformative grace of God. *It* is the story that tells our story, the one that draws us ever onward in faith and hope.

Sometimes it is called "the baptismal covenant." It is the one we are here to remember this morning. In just a few minutes, in the baptismal liturgy, we will be asked to "join with those who are being baptized by reaffirming our baptismal covenant." Then we will proclaim the Apostles' Creed together in one voice. It is my hope this morning that you will say it with gusto, and that our voices will drown out the silly lies that sometimes distract us from this enduring truth. Our lives have been bound to something greater and something better. *Amen.*

THE ULTIMATE GAP-FILLER
(JUNE 4, 2014)

"I commend you to God and to the message of his grace,
a message that is able to build you up." (Acts 20:32)

Our confidence in St. Paul's wisdom and legacy does not
come from the stalwart and tireless effort he showed as a
leader. As the original church planter and overseer of dozens
of new churches, the man himself was spread thin. It's fair
to say that for Paul, there were not enough hours in the day.
His letters are full of apologies related to his inability to visit
each congregation more often. The poor guy was beset with
endless difficulties and constant roadblocks as he journeyed
forward in an attempt to spread the Gospel to the ends of
the earth.

In this evening's reading from Acts, we see these themes
writ large. And in the middle of his address, the Apostle offers some helpful words: "I commend you to God and to the
message of his grace, a message that is able to build you up."
In effect, he is reminding us that Christianity is a religion

primarily of *message,* and not *messenger.*

I used to work at an incredible, James Beard Award winning restaurant in Birmingham, Alabama called The Hot and Hot Fish Club. We served some of the finest food in all of the Southeastern U.S. One of our special dishes was a lamb chili. It had lots of fantastic, fine ingredients, but I remember especially that it contained a secret ingredient. Sure it contained beautiful cuts of meat, the freshest vegetables and beans, and even a few tablespoons of Guinness. But, most importantly, the chef would add a few pieces of bitter dark chocolate to every batch. He said it gave the stew the necessary "depth of flavor" that made it a standout dish.

Where the Christian religion is concerned, we too, following Paul's example, consider ourselves to be the proprietors of a very special ingredient. And it's no secret; it is simply a piece of news, and the news is good: God is in our midst, and He is in the saving business. Christ is our advocate, and the spirit of the God is the breath of life. There is grace enough for every one of us.

If you're feeling spread-thin, or strangely deficient to tackle the tasks that are in front of you, there is hope. Grace is the message, and it will "build you up." You could say that God is in the business of filling in life's gaps, the ultimate and for-all-time gap-filler. In this sense, one might even compare the Gospel to potassium, a single vitamin, which, when it is lacking in a diet, causes all kinds of dysfunction. Yet when it is added to the system that is failing due to its absence, the entire system balances itself out in an overarching and stabilizing kind of a way.

Let me close by sharing one of my favorite depictions of a person who encountered a heaping portion of grace—for there is no other kind—in a most unexpected moment.

The 1946 Academy Award winning movie, *The Best Years of Our Lives*, tells the story of a soldier named Homer. Homer has returned home after a stint away during the Second World War, after losing the lower half of both arms in a submarine explosion. Though he had survived with his humor intact, the return home is marred by embarrassment and pain. With the help of two metal hook-like attachments (and some excellent rehabilitation), he is actually quite high-functioning. But he is convinced that the world now views him as a kind of freak.

The main issue for him is his girlfriend, Wilma. Homer is sure that she will want nothing more to do with him when she sees his "hooks-for-arms." But Wilma is not easily turned away. Her love for Homer appears not to have waned at all. Nonetheless, Homer becomes convinced that she is simply being polite, and that, because of his handicap, they should never be married.

Homer then sets out to sabotage the relationship. He is cold and distracted and pushes away her sweet advances. Finally, late one night, things reach a breaking point. Homer is in the kitchen getting a glass of milk before bed when he looks up to see Wilma standing there at the back door. She says, "Homer, why won't you give me a chance to love you? Do you really want me to go away?"

Homer says, "Let me show you something." He takes her upstairs and says, "Before I crawl into bed, I have to take off my hooks." (And then he removes the holster-like straps that hold them on). He shows her how he can just barely wriggle into his pajama shirt, but he cannot button it. His father has to do that for him each night. He says, "You see, Wilma, at night I'm as helpless as a little baby. What do you have to say to that?" At this point, it's clear that he is expecting her to walk out of the room (and out of his life forever).

Instead, and without even the slightest hesitation, Wilma says, "I know exactly what to say." She picks up the hooks on the bed tenderly, folds the straps, and places them on a chair. Then she comes over to Homer, buttons his shirt for him and says, "Homer, I have always loved you and I still do." And then she kisses him right on the lips. In that touching moment, we see a tear run down the man's cheek, and for the first time since before the war, he puts his little nub of an arm on her shoulder affectionately.

The grace of God is like Wilma's love for Homer. It remains undeterred in its compassionate pursuit. It is bestowed like a gift upon the person toward whom it is focused. It is not merited nor based upon any cost-benefit analysis. It is simply God's heart, beating quietly in the midst of life, just beneath the surface, unwaveringly.

Just as St. Paul reported 2000 years ago with such confidence, the message of grace has the power to build us up. Even you. *Amen.*

FIXED IDENTITY (JUNE 16, 2013)

"But those who were at the table with him began to say among themselves, 'Who is this who even forgives sins?'"
(Luke 7:49)

Today's Gospel lesson tells of a defining moment in Jesus' ministry. We find him at supper, at a rather upscale dinner party, hosted by a prominent local religious leader, Simon the Pharisee. Into the middle of this scene enters a woman of ill repute. She barges into their midst and makes a bit of a scene, anointing Christ's feet with her tears, wiping them with her long hair and slathering them in costly perfume. Simon is not only embarrassed for himself and the intrusion, but also he is embarrassed for Jesus, who would not be associating himself with this woman at all if he knew her reputation. For a man who seemed to have as strong religious convictions as Jesus, an incident like this would surely tarnish that reputation.

But the concerns of Simon do not concern Jesus. And the woman's actions, to him, represent a welcome moment of frank honesty and reality, in the middle of what is otherwise just a dry and phony social outing.

More specifically, we find our Lord addressing two people in this story: Simon, the Pharisee, and the "sinful" woman at his feet. I want to think with you briefly about these two encounters.

First, let's consider the intruder, this woman whose reputation precedes her. She's a known character around town. As one commentator puts it, "Everybody knows who she is, and she's got no hope of ever being any different in anyone's eyes. Her history precludes that... Luke illustrates here a woman bound in an inescapable identity" (J. Stamper). I think those are great words to describe her: "a woman bound in an inescapable identity." To her way of thinking, her role in society, as well as in life, is fixed. She has come to believe about herself, the same thing that everyone else believes about her. As Simon puts it, "she is a sinner."

But I wonder if we cannot show a little empathy this morning. Perhaps there is a point of contact here for each of us. For instance, have you ever felt as though you too were inhabiting "an inescapable identity?" Have you ever been pigeonholed? I often see this kind of thing at play in the world of relationships between siblings. For example, I am the eldest of three boys. My youngest brother, Simeon, has been the butt of jokes related to his low status on the totem pole throughout his life. My brother David and I have seen to it. We have highlighted the fact that Simeon is younger than us, jokingly alluding to the idea that he is some kind of second-tier citizen of our family for most of his life. I remember that at Simeon's wedding, my brother David made a toast in which he basically said, "Okay fine, I'll admit it: Simeon, against all the odds, you've become a man and are ready to get married." It was actually very poignant, because it represented David's attempt to free Simeon from the bonds of a mythology that had, in some sense, come to define and constrain Simeon's life up to that point.

Along these same lines, I wonder: is your inner dialogue subject to some type of mythology? Are you haunted by the way you are and have been regarded by others? Perhaps you're "a neurotic type." Or maybe you're known for being talkative, contrarian, or "always thinking about money." Are you "the cynic," "the control freak," or "the one who abandoned the family," the "the unreliable one?" Maybe you're a "mama's boy" or "the black sheep." Many of us wear multiple hats, but we know and have been taught our roles. Our lives are haunted by these iterations of our character. It may be the case that these identities have been given to you by others and the world at large, or it may be that you've given them to yourself. The chances are that the lines between the two have become blurry and enmeshed.

In the case of the woman in this morning's Gospel, it is clear that she cannot find a way out of her situation. There is no game plan; no way forward that does not involve more of the same. *Status quo* is her only status.

And so it is too with Simon the Pharisee. He represents the other side of the coin. He is the one who enforces the narrative. He is brimming with pride and self-righteousness. He is the snob. Mark Oppenheimer wrote a great confessional piece about snobbery for Slate magazine in 2011 entitled: "The Unholy Pleasure: My life-long recovery from snobbery." In it he confesses:

> "Wherever snobbery can be found, it is evidence of insecurity, even emotional poverty; and yet it is frequently one of life's great pleasures. The problem, of course, is that after a while the snobbery game, like any game played consistently over many years, becomes quite serious... There is no such thing as a recreational snob. The judgmentalism moves to the fore, and the snob really begins to see people as mere butterflies, objects for classification... I do wonder if I can ever change; I cannot decide if I even want to."

He exposes the flip-side of our personalities. Our favorite things about ourselves—like where we went to school, our community-service track record, or our career success—can actually become hindrances to our spiritual well-being. The New Testament makes this point over and over again, that self-righteousness is far more detrimental to the maintenance of a relationship with God than is discouragement or insecurity.

And so it's not hard to see how Jesus displays such high regard for the woman at the bottom. Think of it from her perspective for a moment. Wouldn't it be amazing to get out from under the perceptions that dominate your life, even for just a minute? For her, the possibility is so profound that it causes her to completely break down.

She hears about a man who will love her absolutely and

unconditionally—even her. And so it is too for each of us with God. He is not holding you up against the narrative of your past. Nor is He pinning you down under the stained-glass image of your future. The clipboard has been put away, the presenting issues are completely off the table, and that's where they will stay.

The point of this morning's story is not that things can and will change; it's that we are loved by God *even when they don't*. This is the good news of the Gospel message. *Amen.*

THE ELEPHANT ON THE FRONT PORCH (JUNE 29, 2014)

"Jesus said to him, 'feed my sheep.'" (John 21:17)

This classic passage, on this morning of the Feast of St. Peter and St. Paul, recounts an amazing experience that St. Peter had with the risen Lord. You can imagine the guilt and the anguish that plagued Peter's heart and mind whenever he pondered the moments when he had rejected Jesus so vociferously, just before Christ was taken away to be crucified. "I tell you, I do not know the man!" were his words on that infamous occasion. So then here, on a beach on the Sea of Galilee in Northern Israel, not far from where the two men had had their first encounter three years earlier, Jesus helped Peter to clear the air.

In such circumstances, often people find it easiest to simply skate around the elephant in the middle of the ice rink. They exchange niceties and talk about peripheral matters, avoiding at all costs "the main issue," which is usually a place where there is the vestige of some un-revisited hurt...

and then they part ways, grateful that the awkward (even dreaded) exchange is now over.

It is helpful to note that Jesus does not take this approach with Peter. Instead, he addresses Peter's denial directly ("Do you love me?"), but also (as is always the case with God), he does it tactfully. In case you're not quite sure what I mean, I'm referring to when he asks Peter three times if he loves him. That he does this three times is the key to seeing this dynamic at play. In the same way that Peter had voiced his denial three times, Christ gives him the opportunity to say otherwise three times: "Do you love me? Yes, Lord… Do you love me? Yes, Lord… Do you love me? Lord, you know everything; you know that I love you… Then feed my lambs." It's nuanced, but the redemptive significance is in there for sure.

This second approach to dealing with the elephant on the front porch is, at least in this instance, far more admirable than the first.

I tried both approaches with my wife on the first date that followed a break-up, after we hadn't been in touch at all for six months. Our parting had been a matter of circumstances rather than of apathy or hurt, but our past history and the question mark of whether or not we had a future was glaringly present in that second first date. We agreed to meet for coffee at a local place we had frequented during our first go-round. I remember that the vibe was very tense and nervous. We exchanged lots of glossed-over information: "How are you? I'm good, really good. How are you? Things are great! How's work? Really, that's fantastic! How are your parents? How

are your brothers... Oh really, that's great, really great!..."
Looking back, it was a conversation that got us nowhere. If
anything, it raised more questions than it answered. When
we parted ways after a 45-minute hour, I remember feeling
totally confused and not sure what (of any significance) had
just transpired. There had been so much anticipation.

The result: I called her up two very long days later and
asked if we could meet again, just for a few minutes. Since
acting like everything was fine had failed, our next conversation was much more genuine and succinct. It allowed the
bottled up feelings to burst forth. I told her the truth about
how much I had missed her. She then reciprocated, and it
launched us back into a period of happy courting, followed
by engagement, and now seven years and counting of marriage. I'm still happy about it.

Christ's interaction with Peter that morning gave Peter
a way forward. It gave him a sense of re-instated purpose.
The amazing thing about all of it is that, in fact, it wasn't
a reinstatement at all, but a gracious re-affirmation of the
initial call upon Peter's life. In wake of his poor showing,
perhaps Peter had begun to get the wrong idea about God.
One of my favorite theologians, Robert Capon, put it like
this: "God is not a celestial mother-in-law, giving a glass vase
as a present and then inspecting it for chips every time she
comes for a visit." For Peter, the call remained the same. It
reminds me of that Led Zeppelin song: "The Song Remains
the Same." And such is always the case with grace. It does
not waver in the face of our vicissitudes. It has a steady hand,
always. God's gaze, you see, is full of compassion and not

scrutiny.

The impact that this realization had upon Peter is undeniable. If you know St. Paul's story, you know that he had his own comparable encounter with God's grace, and it blew his mind in a similar fashion. We are gathered here this morning as testaments to their ongoing legacy, and to the long-standing substance of Christ's grace in the world.

On the day they had first met by that same lake, Jesus renamed Simon "Peter," *Petros* in Greek, which means "Rock." Even then, Christ knew that the enduring pronouncement of *forgiveness to back-and-forth types* was destined to become the rock upon which his entire church would be built. It was as though God made an indissoluble vow to Peter on that very first occasion. And the vow held fast, irrespective of Peter's subsequent, checkered performance. Like the words of Ellen Paige in the movie *Juno: "If you're still in, I'm still in."* Or as the Lord himself put it to his disciples, just before the Ascension: "And I will be with you always, even to the end of the age."

It's a sentiment that is reflective of the covenant that God has made with us. In a few minutes, we will baptize two infants. I'm so excited! It represents for them—and for all of us—the reminder that's God's involvement in our lives is born out of the wellspring of cosmic love that Peter experienced in that moment when he was again reminded that he was indeed going to be Christ's successor on earth, the head of the body of Christ, of which we are the living members. *Amen.*

ENEMY-LOVE: A RADICAL NOTION
(JULY 7, 2013)

"You have heard that it was said, 'You shall love your neighbor and hate your enemy.' But I say to you, Love your enemies and pray for those who persecute you..."
(Matthew 5:43-44)

Do you have any enemies? Is anyone actively seeking your demise, hoping your whole life will come to nothing more than a state of complete ruin? I hope the first answer that springs to mind is "no." I certainly doubt that any of you are living in such staunch opposition with your fellow man that an actual plot to bring about your downfall is under way. And this is a good thing to realize on the front end of a sermon about loving one's enemies. We don't really have any, at least not in the extreme sense.

But there's surely a part of us that is inclined to think we do. Are there not people who constantly seem to be getting in your way? Doesn't it sometimes feel as though people are indeed against you? Have you been to the East Bay post office recently, where everything that shouldn't take long takes forever? Have you found that traffic always seems to get much more congested whenever you're in a rush? What about that one particular co-worker who is always making your life more difficult? And let's not even get into family life…

So let me ask: Whom do you resent? Who rubs you the wrong way? If we are to get anything out of this morning's lesson, it's important to realize that these are the people whom Jesus is calling us to love. These people are your (lower-case 'E') enemies.

It's a command that cuts completely against the grain of our instincts. It seems almost otherworldly. To my way of thinking, it is the foreign nature of the command that testifies in part to its divinity.

Notice that Jesus contrasts this idea of enemy-love with a different approach, the more common one, which is "hate" …but let's just call it "distaste." This is the approach that comes easy: We wish for their demise and undoing. We seek to turn others against the people we dislike. We lower our voices, and then we "warn" our friends for the sake of their own well-being, just so that they're "aware of the back-story." We conspire; we avoid; we critique and we shun; or we just look the other way… These are the actions we all know well, and of which Jesus is critical in the extreme.

He suggests that as long as we harbor such feelings towards our enemies, we will know little of what real love is about. *"For if you only love those who love you… and if you greet only your brothers and sisters, what more are you doing than others?"* Love that is based upon merit and reciprociy is not deep love.

In 1979 a French disco artist named Jimmy Senyah released a little-known song called "Weakness for Your Sweetness." (I'm the only person in Charleston who owns a copy of the 45, I suspect.) In it, Jimmy sings to the girl he has a crush on, telling her that he's "got a *weakness* for your *sweetness*." She flutters her eyelashes, and his heart melts. It is because she is so lovely that he loves her. He's got a weakness for her sweetness. But there's a problem with this train of thought. I always wish that I could ask Jimmy, "But what about when she's *not* being sweet?"

Having a weakness for sweetness is not the kind of love that the Gospel teaches, because it is conditional. It's there for you, but only as long as you stay sweet. In such cases, the moment that the chemistry fades, so does the love. Its roots are not deep, and tit-for-tat relationships do not weather adversity well, which is, in truth, the exact thing that love requires.

The point I'm trying to make is that Christianity brings with it the great insight that love has to be grounded in forgiveness if it is going to have any depth or wherewithal. Real love, as Christ reminds us, forgives "seventy times seven."

After years of observing the absence of love in normal human life, I have come to believe that compassion is truly divine. To the extent that I don't have it, my faith calls me to pray that God will bestow more of it to me.

But love is more than a virtue that Christ advocates for each of us to adhere to; it is, most importantly, the kind of love that he has shown the world in dying for you and me, "the righteous for the unrighteous," as St. Paul describes it. How fortunate we are to discover in Scripture the good news, that God loves *us* forgivingly and not according to our merits.

In the Gospel, we learn of a love that is there for us when we are feeling low, stuck, and not very pretty. I'm talking about *"sweetness for your weakness."* In other words, God's love for the enemy includes us in its embrace.

And it's the darndest thing: when we discover that He is there for us in this resolute, won't-be-put-off kind of way, we simultaneously find that we begin to have more patience and treat others more kindly. We become sweeter. If nothing else, hopefully we will no longer justify the absence of compassion that we feel toward our neighbors.

Let me close with an illustration that is not afraid to go all the way with this stuff. It's the story of Mary Johnson and Oshea Israel (which I recently heard on N.P.R'.s *StoryCorps*). Here is an excerpt from the transcript:

> It would be easy—expected, even—for Mary Johnson and Oshea Israel to be enemies. After all, he killed Johnson's only son, in 1993…
>
> As a teenager in Minneapolis, Israel was involved with gangs and drugs. One night at a party, he got into a fight with Laramiun Byrd, 20, and shot and killed him. Oshea is now 34; he finished serving his prison sentence for murder about a year and a half ago.
>
> Israel recently visited StoryCorps with Johnson, to discuss their relationship—and the forgiveness it is

built upon. Johnson recalls, their first face-to-face conversation, "I shared with you about my son."

"And he became human to me," Israel says...

At the end of their meeting at the prison, Ms. Johnson was overcome by emotion, and Israel embraced her. He recounts, "The initial thing to do was just try and hold you up as best I could, just hug you like I would my own mother."

Johnson says, "And after you left the room, I began to say, 'I just hugged the man that murdered my son'.... And I instantly knew that all that anger and the animosity, all the stuff I had in my heart for 12 years for you—I knew it was over, that I had totally forgiven you."

For Israel, Johnson's forgiveness has brought both changes and challenges to his life. "Sometimes I still don't know how to take it," He says, "because I haven't totally forgiven myself yet. It's something that I'm learning from you."

"I treat you as I would treat my son," Johnson says. "And our relationship is beyond belief." In fact, the two live right next door to one another in Minneapolis.

And if he falls out of touch, Israel is sure to hear about it from Johnson—who calls out to him, he says, "'Boy, how come you ain't called over here to check on me in a couple of days? You ain't even asked me if I need my garbage to go out!' "

"I find those things funny, because it's a relationship with a mother for real," Israel says.

"Well, my natural son is no longer here. I didn't see

him graduate. Now you're going to college. I'll have the opportunity to see you graduate," Johnson says. "I didn't see him getting married. Hopefully one day, I'll be able to experience that with you."

Hearing her say those things, Israel says, "It motivates me to make sure that I stay on the right path," He says. "You still believe in me. And the fact that you can do it, despite how much pain I caused you — it's amazing... I love you, lady."

"I love you too, son."

Christ said, "Love your enemies, and pray for those who persecute you." I, for one, believe that he actually meant it. *Amen.*

THE DIFFERENCE BETWEEN LIBERTY AND FREE WILL (JULY 7, 2014)

"For you were called to freedom…" (Galatians 5:13)

I don't know if you remember, but perhaps the Color Guard and the singing of the National Anthem clued you in: Friday was Independence Day. It's an important day in our American identity.

And it is also a feast day observed in our Episcopal liturgical calendar. Did you know that the newly-formed Episcopal Church included the feast in its 1786 prayer book? It was then omitted in 1789. It was taken out upon the recommendation of Bishop William White (who was both the first and fourth Presiding Bishop of The Episcopal Church). He worried that it would alienate former loyalists. In 1928, the Church restored Independence Day as a feast in the updated *Book of Common Prayer*. Episcopal priest and US Navy veteran George Clifford comments on the Church's vacillation in recognizing Independence Day during a sermon on "Fourth of July and the Liturgical Calendar:"

"...the inclusion, omission, and re-inclusion of Independence Day in the liturgical calendar should warn against equating nationalism and Christianity. I hope I don't have to explain that they are not identical. But it is worth noting that during the first century and a half of the Episcopal Church's formation, Episcopalians were careful to view loyalty to Christ and not the nation as paramount."

As I listened from my bed to the fireworks going off last night at midnight, I found myself thinking about some of the ways in which our faith holds this feast in place appropriately.

So can we talk about freedom? What is it exactly? For starters, it is the opposite of captivity. A fair working definition might be: freedom is being able to choose without precondition or constraint.

We are fortunate to live in a country founded upon principles that seek to provide its citizens with a huge amount of freedom. Weekends like this one enable us to bask in gratitude for our many blessings in this regard. Our hymns today, many of them nationalistic, play heavily upon this theme: God has blessed us and provided for us in countless ways. We do well, as always, to reflect today upon all that we have to be grateful for. There are many reasons why it is wonderful to live in the United States of America.

But I want to push back a little on the idea of personal liberty, which is, I think, quite different from national liberty, even though the two are often equated with one another. For example, personal independence is quite different from independence from British governance. And religious freedom is different from individual autonomy. Similarly, opportunity is different from free will.

There are many Christians throughout the ages (including lots of American Christians) who have questioned whether or not human beings are free in and of themselves (*qua* human nature). A few of the more famous proponents of this notion include St. Paul, St. Augustine, Martin Luther, and Thomas Cranmer. All of them voiced a unified skepticism on this front.

St. Augustine suggested that the human will was like a scale of sorts. On one side of the scale was good, and on the other side was bad. He said that, although people like to think that this scale is perfectly balanced, the truth is a bit more grim. He suggested that the scale is weighted in the direction of selfishness—imbalanced, as it were. So with each decision, there is for Augustine, in effect, a bias away from the good. You could say that he felt it was easier to do evil than good, or that people are inclined away from the good by nature. It does not mean that we are incapable of doing good, obviously, and certainly we are capable of wanting to do good—he was not disputing that—but it means that he viewed the doing of good to be harder than its opposite.

Now this notion may sound somewhat unpalatable, but let me ask, is there any truth to it?

In a study conducted a few years ago by Netflix, it was discovered that no DVD spent more time in people's homes than *Hotel Rwanda*. Tons of people rented it, which means that tons of people wanted to see it. It's an important film about important subject matter (the Rwandan genocide). But it stayed in people's homes longer on average than other DVDs in their catalog. In other words, once it arrived, people didn't watch it. They wanted to *have seen* it, but they didn't want to *watch* it. This implies people found it harder to commit to the good they wanted to be a part of than they had anticipated. Many reported returning the movie after many months, never having watched it.

I wonder if there's a place in your own life where the inner scale feels imbalanced, or even permanently stuck, tilted in the wrong direction. Are you a stranger to good intentions that are coupled with "poor execution?" If you can answer no, then allow me to ask: what is this but a lack of freedom in some sense? I know many people who describe themselves as being torn and in the midst of inner conflict for much of their waking lives, who might even say that they are their own worst enemy. Perhaps you've heard the saying from AA: "Every morning, I wake up, look the enemy dead in the eye, and then I shave him."

Aleksandr Solzhenitsyn put it like this:

> "If only it were all so simple! If only there were evil people somewhere insidiously committing evil deeds, and it were necessary only to separate them from the rest of us and destroy them. But the line dividing good and evil cuts through the heart of every human being. And who is willing to destroy a piece of his own heart?"

—*The Gulag Archipelago*, 1918-1956

The Gospel message takes these factors into account, and then it boldly proclaims, not that God loves those who are good, but that God loves people in spite of their failure *to be* good. It proclaims that God has (in Christ) done away with life's bookkeeping and scales altogether. In other words, the Christian religion does not create in people the ability to no longer struggle with making right choices. Instead, it judges them as good—period—regardless of the choices they make.

It is an audacious and radical notion if you think about it. It is even infuriating if you think about how it applies to strangers, for it lets them off the hook scot-free. But if you think for a minute about what it might mean to take this notion on board for yourself, in the midst of your own inner strife (and the endless pressures that you feel heaped upon your shoulders), then for you, this just might be a piece of good news for a change, right in the place where you need it. Being accepted, as such, creates a sense of hope in us that is not unlike new-found freedom. It produces loyalty and humility and gratitude.

One of my professors in seminary spent time in his youth working as a shepherd in Newfoundland. I remember him telling me about one of the common techniques he employed to train young sheep dogs to herd sheep. Apparently, when they start out, sheep dogs are notoriously over-eager. They tend to overrun the sheep and create confusion in the flock. So shepherds loop a large rubber band around their head and one of their front legs, forcing the animal to keep its head close to one of its shoulders. The result is that the dogs are forced to run with a kind of limp. The slight hindrance to their movement keeps the dogs from running too fast, and it trains them quickly, so that after just a few weeks of restraint, the dogs are ready to heard sheep unimpeded.

Sam Shoemaker, the former Rector of Calvary Episcopal Church in New York City, once noted that "Everyone either *has* a problem, *is* a problem, or *lives with* a problem." His point is that we are like those sheepdogs, limping as it were. We are not autonomous, and God will not abandon us entirely unto ourselves, for such is, in truth, life's great recipe for despair. We are not free to serve ourselves, nor have we ever been. But we are free to serve God, whose gracious and sovereign rule we will never escape, a God (as our Prayer Book puts it) "in whose service is perfect freedom." And that is, understandably, cause for celebration. *Amen.*

How to Make a Brain Surgeon
(July 14, 2013)

"But a Samaritan while traveling came near him; and when he saw him, he was moved with pity." (Luke 10:33)

Today we are dealing with Scripture of the highest order.

The parable of the Good Samaritan is one of the most famous bits of the entire Bible. Its fame even rivals passages like the parable of the Prodigal Son, the Sermon on the Mount, and the Lord's Prayer. You can see it, for example, beautifully portrayed on the bronze doors at the entrance of Grace Episcopal Church on Wentworth St. in Charleston, South Carolina (pointing, right there).

To summarize: a young man asks Jesus what life is really all about. It turns out that they both agree in general with what is stated in Old Testament Scripture, that the secret of life in a nutshell has to do with the complete love of God and neighbor. When the man asks him to elaborate upon this second point, about the love of one's neighbor, Jesus tells the following story.

A man was beaten up and left for dead by the side of the road on the outskirts of Jerusalem. Two erudite Jewish men, a priest and a Levite, see the man and quickly cross the street, continuing along on their way. A third guy, a Samaritan, sees the man lying in such a terrible state and is moved. He takes care of him, tending to his wounds and then taking him to an inn where the man can recuperate, generously paying the whole tab and promising to return soon to check in on him.

That's the whole story. It's concise and fairly straightforward. I wish to suggest to you this morning that there are at least two reasons why this parable is so famous. The first is that *its content is universal.* While it certainly benefits a person to know a little bit about Samaritans and Levites, the thrust of the story is intelligible. It's not hard to imagine it in your mind's eye, and one can quickly relate to the issues it raises. The second thing about it is that *it's obviously profound.* It highlights an aspect of life which involves love, one that we all benefit from thinking about. So let's do just that for a few minutes.

Obviously it is the Samaritan's actions in the story that are being lifted up over and against the actions of the other two men (the priest and the Levite), who walk by hurriedly on the other side of the street. Who are these men, and what do we know about them? They are religious men, both of them. One of them serves as a leader in the church, and the other is incredibly well-born. He is most likely a political representative of the Jewish people. They are both by definition associated with holiness and upright living. And yet they both act in an uncharitable fashion.

I'm sure it's the case that the power a person accumulates directly correlates with the amount of attention one receives. When you have power people want to be around you. Certainly, for example, when Jerry Seinfeld ate at The Early Bird Diner on Savannah highway this past Friday, people were more excited about it than they were about the fact that I ate there on Thursday. You can imagine, too, that when people want your attention badly, it creates a level of defensiveness. Famous people put their guard up for understandable reasons. If they have a huge amount of sway, they will even hire bodyguards to act as a buffer between themselves and the world at large.

The priest and the Levite had their guards up, too. It's worth noting that because of ritualistic Jewish laws of purity, if either of these men had gotten blood on their hands, they would be rendered "unclean." This kind of concern played a chief role in their religious observance. Surely the priest and the Levite would have felt it was their duty to avoid touching him for fear of contaminating their righteous status, thereby becoming bad representatives of the things they stood for. Presumably, they may have been rushing to another, in their eyes more important, religious obligation.

But let's not fool ourselves. They were certainly not avoiding the man only for those reasons. They also just didn't want to be bothered. I wonder if you have ever seen some kind of a time-suck headed your way and made quick adjustments in order to dodge it. Have you ever crossed the street, looked the other way, or ducked down in order to avoid conversing with a person at an inopportune moment? We can all relate.

We avoid tedious people, as well as situations that demand huge amounts of our time, in order to preserve the life we seek to build for ourselves. And then, like these two fellows, we find ways to justify those decisions. The priest and the Levite have, in effect, used religious reasoning to explain to themselves why it is okay to act un-lovingly. Perhaps you have witnessed this kind of thing before, an instance where a person cites reasons of virtue to justify some uncharitable action.

There's a story about two lawyers who were walking into the courthouse in Montgomery, Alabama. As they reached the top of the steps to enter the building, a panhandler approached them. One of the lawyers pulled out a five dollar bill and gave it to the man, while the other lawyer looked on with skepticism. When the panhandler was gone, he said, "Why did you give him five dollars? You know he's just going to drink it up." To this, the other man said, *"And if I didn't give him five dollars, are you telling me that he would go on to become a brain surgeon?"*

Christianity is highly critical of the first man's thinking. Unfortunately, the Church has done, and sometimes continues to do, an immense amount of damage in exactly this way, acting unlovingly when exactly the opposite should be the case. Our faith should draw us into greater communion with our neighbors, not further from them. It is a call to engage, where, apart from it, we are inclined not to do so. You can see why we are so quick to encourage a welcoming spirit (especially to the newcomer in our midst) here at Grace Church.

But the Samaritan grasps this. And it's no surprise why, if you know anything about Samaritans. The Samaritans were an ethnic group of people living in Israel who were regarded as outcasts because their Jewish roots were not pure. You see, they were descended from the Jews who had been held captive during the Assyrian captivity. It was believed that most of them were only part-Jewish as a result of intermarriage. Maybe you remember the movie *Blade* with Wesley Snipes, where he plays a "half-breed" who is part human and part vampire? Humans don't want anything to do with him, and the vampires are afraid of him. That's a bit like how the Samaritans were treated. Jews were told not to have anything to do with them. Do you remember when Jesus speaks with the Samaritan woman at the well? Her first question to him is basically, "What are you doing talking to me, since I'm a Samaritan?" And then also the first question the disciples ask when they see him talking with her: "What are you doing talking with her? Can't you see she's a Samaritan?!"

And so perhaps you can begin to piece together why it is that the Samaritan was so ready to act compassionately toward the downtrodden man in the ditch. Unlike the priest and the Levite, the Samaritan could identify. He knew exactly what it was like to be avoided, to have people mistreat you. And he could understand what it is like to be beaten down by life.

I wonder if you too have a place in your own life where you have been beaten down? Or maybe you have some kind of besetting weakness or stigma? I bet that it is to that exact extent that you have compassion for people going through similar situations, because you can understand them better than people who do not know what it's like.

Here we find in this parable a great insight, that *compassion and understanding are closely interwoven*. In my experience of pastoral care, I find that *when a person feels that they have been understood, they also feel loved*. It's no wonder the best counselors are often people who have themselves needed counsel at one point or another. And just to be clear, the parable of the Good Samaritan reminds us that this kind of understanding and compassion is *Good*; it is what life is all about, the place where meaning and purpose and existence intersect.

Finally, I would be remiss if I didn't point out that we are here this morning primarily because of the one who completely identified with the downtrodden and the outcast. The people in power rejected him, and then he was beaten and left to die. He is the one who knows better than anyone else what it's like to be mistreated, who knows what it's like to be on the outside looking in. And not surprisingly, we find in him the compassion of the Good Samaritan, the willingness to be taken in by whatever is weighing you down. He is the one who was often called, "the friend of sinners" and "the man of sorrows." He has time for you and will attend to your needs.

It's no wonder people saw in Christ true godliness, which is mercy and complete understanding, which is love. *Amen.*

1,112 (JULY 21, 2013)

"But Martha was distracted by her many tasks..."
(Luke 10:40)

In honor of Martha, I feel it is my duty to ask: Do you have a to-do list? What's on your list? I can remember not so many years ago, scribbling my to-do list down on the back of my bulletin while sitting in church. It was one of the only places where I could get a quiet moment. It was in the quiet of worship that my brain seemed always to wander back to all of the things I needed still to do, all of the unfinished aspects of my life, the "things left undone," to quote the *Book of Common Prayer*.

I don't think I'm the only one with a brain like this, one who is constantly crossing things off of an endless mental list and also constantly adding new items to this same list. In fact, I know I'm not, because I find in Martha, two thousand years ago in the near-Eastern region of Palestine, a kindred spirit. There is no doubt that Martha would appreciate the fact that there are actually 1,112 to-do list apps available on the iPhone at this point in history. Do you ever find your-self to be like dear Martha, worrying anxiously about all the things you need to do? Do those things distract you? Let me overstate this idea, just to be clear: are you a slave to your to-do list?

It is into the middle of these distractions that Jesus speaks these famous words: *"you are worried and distracted by many things; [but] there is need of only one thing."* There is only one "needful thing." Jesus suggests that there is one single ingre-dient that causes all of the other elements of life to fall into place. There is a sure foundation, a rock upon which we can build. That place is found in God, for it is faith.

Perhaps you are familiar with the theological distinction that is sometimes drawn between *the vertical* and *the horizon-tal.* "The vertical" represents the place of looking up toward God, the place in our hearts where we ask for help and try our best to trust in heavenly guidance and the provision that comes from above. And then there is "the horizontal plane," all that we see in front of us, to our left and our right, the details on the ground, the endless incidentals. To neglect this vertical aspect of our existence is to miss out on life's truest foundation. No expenditure of effort and no caliber of per-formance can provide its substitute.

A friend of mine described the nature of this distinction to me recently, as we were sitting in his living room. He was telling me about his dog. He said, "My dog thinks that all of this belongs to him. *The truth is that none of it does.*"

Jesus' words for Martha are words also for you and me. He tells us that it is the vertical perspective on life that enables us to make sense and rise to the occasion of the endless tasks that punctuate our horizontal endeavors. It is faith that enables us to face our lives with confidence. Not because we know what will happen, but because we find assurance in the One who does. It is the one thing that is needful. "Seek ye first the kingdom of God, and all else shall be given to you." *Amen.*

THE PEANUT BUTTER SHUFFLE
(JULY 24, 2013)

"...and the last will be first." (Matthew 19:30)

In this evening's Gospel lesson, the mother of two of the disciples, James and John, comes to Jesus and asks that her sons be given special treatment. I'm not sure, but I don't think she's the first parent in history to do something like this. She wishes for her children, as do all parents, that they'll become successful in the avenue of life in which they have invested themselves. And so, if her sons are going to be "disciples" for a living, then she wishes for them to become the most successful disciples in Jesus' camp.

Unfortunately, she betrays a complete misunderstanding of the faith to which her sons have committed themselves. Her intentions are both sweet and perhaps also a little self-serving, not unlike the grandmother who happily touts the fact that her "grandson is a freshman at Harvard." Unfortunately for her, and for all of us, this train of thought is worldly in the extreme.

191

The problem for her, which she soon discovers from the answer she is given, is that Christian thought tends to flip worldliness on its head. It doesn't just renounce the ultimate importance of material trappings and pedigree; it also lifts up the importance of the things of life which we tend to shy away from. As Christians, for example, we value humility over and against pride. We like sacrifice better than accomplishment. And we choose each other before we choose ourselves. If we apply this material to the worlds of football and basketball (something that I am not all that well-equipped to do), it might mean that the only team we should ever root for is that of the underdog. Christ tells us, "whoever wishes to be great among you must be your servant, and whoever wishes to be first among you must be your slave." Christ is arguably the strongest counter-example to The American Dream ever described in history.

It reminds me of a game we used to play at the Christian summer camp I attended as a child. It was called "the peanut butter shuffle." When it came time for us campers to line up for lunch, it would be announced that we were going to be making our own PB&Js. We would hustle up to the picnic bench, hungry and eager to get our rations. Once we were lined up, the counselor would announce that "Today we're going dance a little dance called 'the Peanut Butter Shuffle.'" Then they would tell us to stay in single-file formation while we boogied and jived behind the counselor at the front of the line, following his lead. We would shimmy our way forward, slowly making our way past the sandwich station, until eventually the last person in the line was standing next to the sandwich goods, at which point we were told to make a 180-degree about-face. It was then announced that the shuffle was over, and that today "the last were going to be first," that the boy who had been at the back of the line was now at its front, with the line-leader now the caboose. You get the idea...

But I'm talking about this passage all wrong, as though we are the ones on top of the pile, people who may or may not choose to place ourselves at the back of the line from here on out. Would that we were so "ambitious." But the Bible's story is not a story about the person who is at the front of the line and what he or she will or won't do with that opportunity. It's a story about the only one who ever rightly occupied, or could have occupied, that position. It's a story about what he did for the sake of the rest of us, all of whom are behind him.

You see, you don't have to shift much at all in order to find yourself at the back of the line. All you have to do is think about where you stand in relationship to God and to life and to all the standards that you and the world have set for you. There is *only* the back of the line for people like you and me, unless we have begun to kid ourselves about the many gifts we have been given. As Paul puts it, "If anyone thinks he is something when he is nothing, he deceives himself."

The only extent to which you and I excel in any capacity is the extent to which God's grace has made itself evident in our lives. And, furthermore, the places in our lives that are broken and destitute and sagging and under huge amounts of pressure, well... take comfort; those are also the places where our God is found to be most profoundly at work, the places where He lives and reigns. Those are the aspects of life that only a God of love could find great value in. But that is what makes the Gospel so sweet. The love of Christ covers a multitude of sins, providing, as he puts it in tonight's lesson, "a ransom for many."

Finally, let me close with a favorite description of the re-orientation of perspective that comes from faith. It is taken from one of the basic texts of Alcoholics Anonymous called *The Twelve Steps and Twelve Traditions*. Listen to these words from AA's founder, Bill W., who knew all about life on the bottom of the pile, and how the grace of God can make use of just such a circumstance. He writes:

> "Still more wonderful is the feeling that we do not have to be specially distinguished among our fellows in order to be useful and profoundly happy. Not many of us can be leaders of prominence, nor do we wish to be. Service, gladly rendered, obligations squarely met, troubles well accepted or solved with God's help, the knowledge that at home or in the world outside we are partners in a common effort, the well-understood fact that in God's sight all human beings are important, the proof that love freely given surely brings a full return, the certainty that we are no longer isolated and alone in self-constructed prisons, the surety that we need no longer be square pegs in round holes but can fit and belong in God's scheme of things—these are... permanent and legitimate satisfactions... for which no amount of pomp and circumstance, no heap of material posses-

sions, could possibly be substitutes. True ambition is not what we thought it was. *True ambition is the deep desire to live usefully and humbly under the grace of God*" (p. 125).

Amen.

WHO CAN IT BE NOW?
(JULY 28, 2013)

"Suppose one of you has a friend, and you go to him at midnight...." (Luke 11:5)

This morning's Gospel reading deals with prayer. Jesus gives us the shortened Lukan version of the Lord's Prayer, which is notably succinct. He then tells the parable of the friend at midnight, in which a man shows up at a buddy's house in the middle of the night, banging on the door and requesting some supplies, because he is ill-equipped to deal with an unexpected circumstance. Then Jesus mentions that God answers prayers with a most impressive sensitivity. He underscores the fact that our heavenly Father answers prayers in a way that is full of goodness and prudence, and that these responses are full of compassion.

So, bearing that little synopsis in mind, I want to focus on the image of prayer that we are given in the parable. First, let us deal with what it is *not* saying, and how this passage has sometimes been misinterpreted. Then we'll consider what remains, hopefully arriving at a better understanding of prayer.

The parable of the friend at midnight has sometimes been thought to be about persistence in prayer. People have sometimes concluded from this reading that the secret to prayer lies in persistence and that to the extent that your prayers have not been answered in a way that seems adequate, you just haven't prayed hard enough, or carefully enough, or in the right way. This is a dangerous train of thought and one of which we need to be disabused.

Life experience makes it abundantly clear that suffering cannot necessarily be wiped away with the help of prayer. I have yet to meet a single Christian who does not suffer. One can only imagine how many sincere and unceasing prayers have been uttered up to God from the rooms of MUSC's Children's Hospital, for example. The hard truth about prayer is that it has very little to do with control.

Whether we like it or not, prayer just doesn't work that way. Prayers which do not develop into palatable and pleasant outcomes do not have to do with faults found in the individual who prays them. In many respects, it is prayer that forces us to accept the facts on the ground as we lift up the desires of our hearts and share with God how we would prefer for things to be. But let's be clear: the Christian religion is not voodoo; it has little to do with the manipulation of circumstances, but lots to do with the relinquishing of those ideas. Faith is not about trusting God to do the thing you want Him to do; it is about trusting Him when you have absolutely no idea where God is or what He is doing.

On the other side of this misinterpretation, we are given a concrete image of prayer in this morning's parable. It has to do with the guy who shows up banging on his friend's door in the middle of the night. Jesus notes in verse 8 that it is because of the man's "persistence," which is a word also translated as "impudence" or "shamelessness," that the host in turn gives the man what he needs, in spite of the circumstances.

And what are the circumstances? What do we know about the man doing the knocking?

Well, for one thing, it's the middle of the night. I wonder, when was the last time you knocked on someone's door at midnight? I remember knocking on the door of a farmhouse in rural Ohio after I rolled my friend's Subaru Outback into a cornfield at 2 a.m. one November. We all know that the situations which involve late-night knocking are pretty dire. Otherwise, we wouldn't do a thing like that. In a similar vein, think of how a parent responds to a late-night phone call. You know it's important if it's happening at an inopportune moment.

And so we see that prayer finds its voice in the face of difficulty. It is born out of stress and confusion. Real prayer is nervous. Are you stressed about anything this morning? Or perhaps it's better to ask, were you stressed about anything in the middle of the night last night? Please know that this is a call to prayer, and a reminder that you cannot do life well without leaning upon God's grace. Prayer opens us up to the answers that we cannot see coming and to the hope we cannot make sense of until it has come upon us. Prayer is the thing which opens us up to see the work of God in our lives, and it often happens when events have forced us into a position of humility. Prayer is the reminder that we need to loosen our grip on life.

In my own life, I experienced this in a pronounced way during my first year out of college. My relationship with my college girlfriend was eroding, and I prayed a very honest prayer: "Dear Lord, please don't let her leave." I believe God heard my prayer that day. And then, a few weeks later, she dumped me. I'll also never forget the callous words my friend Nick offered me at the time. He said, "One day you'll thank God you didn't marry that girl!"

But Nick was right. I remember thinking on my wedding just how grateful I was that my prayers had been answered in that way, and that I had not been given the opportunity to marry a spouse who would not have been right for me. God's "no" turned out to be an upgrade the likes of which I still marvel at!

Do note the good news, too, that God responds with compassion. He is not like me: Deirdre and I don't answer our door after midnight as a rule. Thank God that God is not like the Zahls in this respect. As the great Robert Capon once put it, "This parable gives us the assurance that God is a light sleeper. Like Motel 6—he'll 'leave the light on for you'—the door is always open."

I have seen prayers answered in countless ways, with "Yes," with "No," with "Soon" and with "Later." And I have no doubt that prayer changes things, especially because of the way it changes us. Prayer reorients our perspective and puts us in a position where we can do that thing that people don't usually like to do, which is *receive*. I've seen prayers answered with water turning into wine, and I've seen prayer enable people to slog through the most difficult and unrelenting circumstances without them becoming their undoing. I've seen it enable people to change their entire way of dealing with a frustrating person, and I've seen it bring about transformation in the most rigid and un-budging brokenness. It is life's secret ingredient.

Let me close with some more words which Robert Capon wrote about this passage. They summarize what I have been trying to say.

> "Taken literally as a program for conning God into catering to the needs of our lives, that is pure bunk: too many sincere, persistent prayers have simply gone unfulfilled. But taken as a command constantly to bring our deaths to his death and to find our resurrection in his, well, then it's solid gold."

Amen.

DON'T WORRY, JESUS IS ANGRY
(AUGUST 18, 2013)

"They tie up heavy burdens, hard to bear, and lay them on the shoulders of others..." (Matthew 23:4)

Jesus has no harsher things to say in his entire ministry than the pointed critiques which he continually lobs at the Pharisees. They were the ruling religious class of Jewish church leaders at that time, people who appealed to the same Old Testament texts that Christ himself valued so deeply. While he also displayed a distaste for those Jewish leaders who played a role in the political life of the people of Israel, the Sadducees, it was the Pharisees who drew the majority of Jesus' ire.

We do well to ask why it was that he found the Pharisees to be especially off-putting. Obviously, Jesus did not dislike all of them as individuals, willy-nilly, for we must remember that Nicodemus was a Pharisee, and also a man whom Jesus cared for and respected. You may remember that it was Nicodemus who saw to it that Jesus received a proper burial.

No, it was not the Pharisees as individuals whom Jesus had a problem with; it was the ideas about religion which they advocated and the way he felt that they misled the people of God in their ministry to them. In his view, they had perverted true religion, trying to build their security on commandments that can only, at the end of the day, convince us of our need for mercy. But the love part, the part we call the grace of God, which is the sure foundation of our faith, well, that bit seemed to be missing entirely from their teachings.

In the 23rd chapter of Matthew's Gospel, Jesus explains this reasoning in very clear terms. He says:

> "They tie up heavy burdens and lay them on men's shoulders, but they themselves are unwilling to move them with so much as a finger. But they do all their deeds to be noticed by men... They love the place of honor at banquets and the chief seats in the synagogues, and respectful greetings in the market places, and being called Rabbi by men... Whoever exalts himself shall be humbled; and whoever humbles himself shall be exalted."

It's an understandable critique. Not only are the Pharisees self-deceived—using spiritual terminology to justify their own self-serving endeavors—they are inflicting their misguided religious understanding upon the lives of others, the people in the pews who, in effect, find themselves to be "carrying burdens" as a result.

And the Christian religion is, after all, all about the laying down of burdens, not the carrying of them. The church is a place where trespasses are met with forgiveness and where absolution is trumpeted from on high, no strings attached. The church which misses this simple point of emphasis is a church which has lost its way.

Furthermore, the Christian faith is not an avenue by which we can seek to justify our prideful inclinations but, rather, the exact opposite: it is the place where we seek to become humble before God and our fellow human beings. Pride is indeed a thing that stands in the way of our spiritual growth, a thing which keeps us from engaging with the goodness of our Creator.

May I ask: where have cocksureness and arrogance distorted your view of things? Where have you come to believe you are justified by your own efforts, and not the loving efforts of the one who died with all of the world's burdens (including yours) on *his* back?

Remember his most comfortable words: *"Come unto me, all ye who travail and are heavy-laden, and I will give you rest."*
Amen.

CHOICE FOOD AND SWEET (TEA)
(JANUARY 24, 2010)

"And Nehemiah... said to all the people, '...Do not mourn and weep.' For all the people wept when the heard the words of the law. Then he said to them, 'Go your way, eat the fat and drink sweet wine... and do not be grieved.'" (Nehemiah 8:9-11)

If you want to summarize the theme of Nehemiah in a word, it's about "restoration." Then again, isn't that what Christianity is all about? It's the theme at the heart of our message, and so it's not surprising that we encounter it once again today. I hope I can breathe some life into it for you.

This guy, Nehemiah, was a Jew who served in the Persian government as a cupbearer when Israel was in a terrible state of disrepair. The people of Israel had become captives to foreign rule, and their spirits were low. Nehemiah became especially saddened when he heard about the state of the holy city, Jerusalem. After a period of prayerful consideration (and anguish), he told the Persian emperor all about it. Obviously the Persian emperor liked Nehemiah, because he said to him, in effect: "You know what? You can go back to Jerusalem. Try to restore it. Try to bring life back to a city that that is dying."

And so Nehemiah traveled back to Jerusalem and, famously, rebuilt the walls of that decaying city. But not only did he repair the edifice—he also brought the word of God back to the people. The passage that we read this morning describes the reaction they experienced when the Biblical word was reintroduced to them.

It reminds me of the story of a friend of mine who didn't go to church for 35 years. One day his wife figured out a way to get him to visit the church she had been attending during much of his prolonged "sabbatical." He walked in and heard something there. He says he doesn't remember what the words of the sermon were, but he does remember that they conveyed something that he had been missing, an enabling word from God. It was a kind of homecoming. Apparently he has only missed four 8 a.m. services since then. It's a perfect portrait of a person who is not coming to church because he is trying to make up for a 35-year absence; he's coming because he found something in church that makes all the difference in life, and he'd forgotten about it.

And that's exactly what happened with these people here in Nehemiah. So I want to look at it. But before I do, let me just point out that it's very easy to get trapped in a kind of downward spiral. You don't go one week, you don't go two weeks, you don't go three weeks, and then, suddenly, five years have gone by. Or, for another example, you start to not like somebody, and then five seconds later you hate them forever. And then it becomes easy to move to a new city, just so that you won't have to see that person ever again. Do you see how quickly things in our lives can get entrenched? It doesn't take long, and I hope that you'll see that these people were just like us in that regard.

In the same vein, Deirdre and I have this new car that has a tire pressure light. What a great thing: an exclamation point lights up on the dash whenever the pressure in one of the tires gets low. The first time the light went on, I made a beeline for an air pump, thinking that I might not even be able to make it to the gas station (one mile away) before the tire was flat. But when I got out of the car next to look, I couldn't even tell which one was low. They all looked full. The sensor, it turns out, is very sensitive. Now it's gotten to the point where, when the light pings on, I think to myself, "meh... can't be bothered to take care of it today. It won't be flat for a few months." And so I just ride around with a big exclamation point illuminated on the dash. Some of you may remember The Cure, my old favorite band from high school. I used to love them. The lead singer, Robert Smith, sang in one of their songs: "the further I get from the things that I care about, the less I care about how much further away I get." And that's the situation that God is up against, in all of our lives, every day of the week. It's also the situation with the Israelites in this morning's reading. A long time has gone by, and they're in much worse shape even than they realize. So then, let's look at what happens.

The word of the Lord is opened up to them. It's taught to them by Ezra, a priest. And when he finishes reading the words of the Law, they respond, "Amen, Amen," words that draw out just how touched and impacted they were upon hearing this teaching. "Then they bowed down and worshiped the Lord with their faces to the ground." They were prostrate. This is not a picture of joyful worship and glorious praise. It's a description of repentance and of manifest regret. Look a little further down. The priest comes out and attacks them all, saying, "You've been a long way from where you need to be for a long time. You are unscrupulous moral failures!" And the hearers feel convicted.

It's important to notice the difference between the priest's approach and the tone of the governor, Nehemiah's words, which follow them. Keep in mind too that he had the vision for this whole enterprise in the first place. The people are bowed down, feeling laid low, when Nehemiah, the big daddy, comes out. And his words are the final word. He says, "Do not mourn and weep" (because that's what they were doing when their lives were finally held up to the mirror of God's standard). And a little further on, Nehemiah says, "*Do not grieve, but go and enjoy choice food and sweet drink.*"

We'll return to the value of Nehemiah's contribution shortly, but before we do, let's talk a little more about what it means to be headed on a one-way ticket out the door. I recently saw a movie called The Box. It's sort of a weird movie, based on a short story by Richard Matheson, who also wrote for The *Twilight Zone*. And there was a *Twilight Zone* episode in the 50s that this movie was based on, called "Button Button." *The*

Box was made by the same guy who directed Donnie Darko. Cameron Diaz is the only famous person in it.

Early one morning a normal, average family hears a knock at their front door. When they open it, they find on their doorstep a box with a little card. And they open the plain brown paper wrapping to find a cherry-wood box that has a glass lid. Under the lid, which is on hinges, there's a big red button, like the kind of button you imagine would need to be pushed if you wanted to launch a nuclear warhead. Confused, they then open the card, which reads, "Mr. Stevens will be by later to explain what this is about."

A little while later, the doorbell rings, and a man with an awful visage—his face appears to be half-burned all across the right side—is standing there. But he's very well-dressed and has pulled up in a Rolls-Royce. They invite him into their home. He walks in and sits down across from the couple, with the box in between them. And he says, "Here's the deal. You have 24 hours to decide if you want to push this button. If you push it, someone that you do not know will die, and you will receive one million dollars, tax-free, in cash." He then opens a briefcase, showing them the money, and hands them a one-hundred dollar bill for their trouble, regardless of the decision they choose to make. And he leaves.

Well, what do you think happens? After tons of deliberation, weighing all of the options, they do it. Not only that, but by the time they do it, they have completely justified the decision, telling themselves that it's very much the right thing to do. After all, they could use the money, and they're sure that no one in their right mind would come up with a deal like this if the person who was to die was not actually being put out of some misery. They wrestle with it throughout the night, and early the next morning—boom—they push the red button. And someone dies whom they do not know.

A few minutes later, the man comes by. He gives them the briefcase full of cash and takes the box, saying he must be on his way... to the next house. Immediately following this, their lives completely unravel. It has, in fact, set a bunch of awful things in motion, most of which are internal. The couple is hugely drawn apart as the husband continues to justify the decision they've made, while the wife is consumed by remorse.

Cameron Diaz's character eventually tracks down the scary Mr. Stevens, who represents personified evil, like a devil figure. She tells him: "If I had known what would happen, I never would've pushed the button!" In a chilling response, he says, "They *always* push the button. *Everyone always pushes the button.*" The point is that people in a bind can always justify self-interest over and above love of their neighbor. In fact, our default as human beings—if the curtains are closed and nobody's watching, and we think we can get away with it—is, "hate thy neighbor." It's "kill they neighbor."

This is a heavy insight, but one that we can learn from. You've probably experienced small expressions of deep-seated self-involvement in all kinds of unexpected moments. One might, for example, choose the bigger ice cream portion by taking two bites from the ice cream container so that the portions look the same when they're presented. Why else, after all, would a person volunteer to serve dessert in the first place?

Scripture is no stranger to these types of under-handed motives. In *The Box*, when Cameron Diaz finally confronts Mr. Stevens at the end of the film, she says, "Isn't there any way that I can be forgiven?" She understands, given human nature, that the only way out of that cycle has to be forgiveness. But his answer is heartless. He says, "I'm sorry, but that's not the way this works." And then he walks off, and their lives are completely destroyed.

The good news for us is that in Christianity, that *is* "the way this works." Notice what Nehemiah says to these button-pushing types:

> "Then Nehemiah, the governor, pushed [the legalistic] preacher out of the way, and said, 'Do not mourn or weep.' For all the people had been weeping as they listened to the words of the Law. 'Do not grieve, for the joy of the Lord is your strength. Go and enjoy choice food and sweet drinks.'"

This is an expression of the tone of the enabling word of the Gospel message. We find it clearly professed in this morning's Collect from the *Book of Common Prayer*: "Give us grace to proclaim to all people the good news of Thy salvation."

That's what we're talking about here this morning: the good news of salvation, which is the forgiveness of sins. It's why we put a cross at the center of our worship.

In closing, let me tell you a story I heard recently that blew me away. I have been given permission to share it.

One of the members of our church was left in the care of her three capable older siblings when she was eleven years old, because her parents had to leave town for a few days. Just minutes after she saw them head to the airport, a sneaky idea popped into her head. She went inside and took her mother's car keys in a moment when nobody was looking. For what it's worth, she had experience driving the family's riding lawnmower. Anyway, she climbed into the front seat and turned on the car, put it in reverse, and proceeded to back out of the driveway. She then drove up to her best friend's house, just up the street, picked up her friend, and did what any free-thinking eleven-year-old would do— headed straight for McDonald's.

And on the way to McDonald's, in a surreal moment, she passed her aunt, this girl's mother's sister, who was very much not out of town. Quickly, the dots were connected and the aunt realized what she'd just seen, and this girl realized what she'd just been seen doing. So she turned the car right around and drove straight back home... where she found her three older siblings waiting for her in the driveway. They were not amused.

She spent the next few days like Cinderella, doing everybody's chores and being reminded that she was in trouble. But the girl never heard from her parents directly in the interim, though she was told they had been informed about what had happened. As a side-note, in this story, her mom is kind of a Nehemiah proxy, and her siblings are the Ezra stand-ins.

Apparently her mother told her later, "I prayed a lot about what do with you when I got home, about how I could best handle this situation." Here's what she did. She came home, and when she saw her daughter, she said, "Honey, did you ever make it to McDonald's? Let's go." And just the mom and the daughter went off, and they had at a little meal together at McDonald's. It's very touching.

Forgiveness is the only thing that can really deal with the Law's demands. We will all continue to struggle with the un-evangelized territories of our souls, where we continue to push the button at various points in our lives. But the surprise of grace, which is the Gospel message, will continue to sweeten the pot called "sinner's stew" to the end of the ages. And the darkness will not overcome it. *Amen.*

WHEN ALL OTHER APPROACHES FAIL
(SEPT. 7, 2014)

"'If another member of the church sins against you, go and point out the fault when the two of you are alone... But if you are not listened to, take one or two others along with you, so that every word may be confirmed by the evidence of two or three witnesses. If the member refuses to listen to them, tell it to the church; and if the offender refuses to listen even to the church, let such a one be to you as a Gentile and a tax-collector.'"
(Matthew 18:15-17)

Consider the following quote from Aldous Huxley: "There is no such thing as a conscious hypocrite." Now put that in the back of your mind as we look at this morning's Gospel lesson. We'll revisit what I think Mr. Huxley is getting at in a few minutes.

This morning's Gospel, taken from Matthew 18, outlines a three-fold method for dealing with problems in the church. It says that "when a person sins against you," the first thing to do is to go to the person, confront them about it and try to resolve the issue smoothly behind closed doors. If that fails to bring forth penitence in the guilty party, it is suggested that you, should then go back to the person with a vestry member (or two). If the second visit yields no further progress, then, third, we are advised to address the issue publicly (for example, in a church forum).

I must report that this is not one of my favorite passages from Scripture. Personally, I'm a bit skeptical about the method as being one which gets through to the offending party. There are three reasons for this. First, the third suggestion seems to endorse a kind of public shaming, which I think can be cruel and damaging. Second, the efficacy of this method is a bit dubious. The recent scandal surrounding mega-church pastor, Mark Driscoll in Seattle, is a perfect example of an instance where these methods were tried and seemed to do more harm than good. But the main reason I take issue with Matthew 18 is because Christians have been known to appeal to it in an attempt to justify acting unforgivingly, which, I think, flies in the face of so much of the rest of Christian teaching.

The approach outlined seems to work well, perhaps, for protecting an institution, and as a final measure (which is the underlying reason for its having been suggested), but the method rarely gets through to the person being addressed. Think of how few interventions work, and how often our attempts to get people to fall in line backfire.

Most people are facing an inner problem in these types of circumstances, when they have become the offending party. It is the problem of self-justification. Matthew 18 does a good job of drawing attention to this aspect of human nature. It's always there, but it doesn't boldly rear its head until we get caught out for having made a mistake.

A great book was written about this a few years ago, called *Mistakes Were Made (But Not By Me).* In it, the authors describe the problem:

> Self-justification is not the same thing as lying or making excuses… there is a big difference between what a guilty man says to the public to convince them of something he knows is untrue ("I did not have sex with that woman;" "I am not a crook"), and the process of persuading himself that he did a good thing. In the former situation, he is lying and knows he is lying to save his own skin. In the latter, he is lying to himself. That is why self-justification is more powerful and more dangerous than the explicit lie. It allows people to convince themselves that what they did was the best thing they could have done… Self-justification not only minimizes our mistakes and bad decisions; it is also the reason that everyone can see a hypocrite in action except the hypocrite.
>
> By understanding the inner workings of self-justification, we can… make sense of dozens of [the] things that people do that would otherwise seem unfathomable or crazy. We can answer the question so many people ask when they look at ruthless dictators, greedy corporate CEOs, religious zealots who murder in the name of God, or people who cheat their siblings out of a family inheritance: How in the world can they live with themselves? The answer is: exactly the way the rest of us do.

The psychologist Kathryn Schultz builds upon these ideas in her own work. In her famous TED Talk, based largely upon material found in her book *Being Wrong*, she comments:

> "In the present tense, I can't actually bring to mind anything that I'm wrong about... we all travel through life feeling trapped in little bubble of feeling very right about everything."

She asks the crowd, "How does it feel to be wrong?" And they answer, thumbs down, dreadful, embarrassing, devastating, etc... Schultz then points out that they've answered a different question than the one actually she asked. They've told her how it feels to *realize* you're wrong about something... but, as she says, "just being wrong doesn't feel like anything." Referencing the famous Road Runner cartoon, she continues: "when we're wrong about something, we're like that coyote after he's run off the cliff, but before he looks down... we're already wrong, we're already in trouble, but we feel like we're on solid ground." Correcting her earlier statement, "It actually does feel like something to be wrong... *It feels like being right.*"

The truth is that self-justification is wily and seemingly inescapable. The depressing thing is that this passage, at face value, seems ultimately to ostracize all wrong-doers who fail to recognize their wrongdoing. It only draws out the gravity of their impediment.

But that's where the most important verse in the entire passage comes in. Did you notice it, there toward the end? "If such a one refuses to listen even to the church, let such a one be to you as a Gentile and a tax collector."

It's a fascinating statement, and one which actually doubles back on everything that has been said up until this point.

What does it mean for the church to "be [to the offender] as a Gentile and a tax collector"? It means, *at the point where nothing else is getting through, it's time to try grace.* Think of how Jesus treated the tax-collector, Zacchaeus. Remember how Peter baptized an entire Gentile household, or how Jesus engaged with the Samaritan woman at the well?

Grace seems to work when and where nothing else has worked. Grace is designed primarily to handle repeated and egregious offense. Of course, it is precisely because of self-justification that protective measures like the ones described in this passage have to be taken. But when the concern shifts from the preservation and protection of oneself, to concern for the one who is living in problematic delusion, a forgiving love becomes crucial. It doesn't necessarily do away with the consequences that have to be meted out, but grace reaches out to the heart that seems impenetrably far-gone.

I watched a television documentary about the trial of a man named Gary Ridgway, who committed a string of atrocious crimes. During his trial, a string of his victims' families were given an opportunity to address him. They gave voice to their pain and anger, saying things like, "You deserve a slow and painful death." "You're an animal!" "You're going to hell which is where you belong." Throughout the trial, Gary sat completely stone-faced with a horrifying, sociopathic detachment, as the atrocities he had committed were recounted. Even when devastated family members voiced their heart-break, the perpetrator displayed zero emotion, just a blank stare.

Then an old man with a long white beard and rainbow suspenders approached the microphone. He said, "Mr. Ridgeway, you've made it difficult to live up to what I believe, which is what God says to do, and that's to forgive. There are people here that hate you... I am not one of them. You are forgiven, sir." With those words, Gary Ridgeway lowered his head, and tears streamed down his face.

Similarly, in the case of each of us, in the place where we are wrong and deluded, God's grace is the final word. It is the place where we discover "a peace that passes understanding," which is heavenly absolution. *Amen.*

ABREACTION AND LIFE IN ALLEGORY (SEPT 8, 2013)

"Just like the clay in the potter's hand, so are you in my hand..." (Jeremiah 18:6)

Jeremiah had the profound experience of hearing God speak to him. He saw, in an image from life, a meaning that spoke to him about the ways of the Lord.

The 5-dollar word in psychology for this is "abreaction," which is defined as a moment when one's life suddenly connects with a much deeper universal truth through the means of an allegory. It often happens to people as they watch movies or read books, when they suddenly find themselves identifying with the characters. Perhaps this has happened to you at some point.

The image that so deeply connected with Jeremiah is one that we all do well to consider. One day, he came upon a potter who was working on some clay. We read:

"So I went down to the potter's house, and there he was

223

working at his wheel. The vessel he was making of clay was spoiled, so he was reworking it into another vessel as seemed good to him."

Let's reflect together upon this story. Here we encounter two main elements: there is the potter, and then there is the clay. As you know, a potter works with clay. The clay is taken from the ground and used to create beautiful objects, objects which typically serve important functions.

In this allegory, it is suggested to us that God is like the potter, and that we are like the clay in His hands. It's a suggestion that simultaneously offends and comforts.

The offense comes from the suggestion that we, being clay, ultimately serve the vision of the potter. We, in effect, are not the potter. For the more Type A aspects of our personalities, this comes as an affront. Was William Ernest Henley really wrong? Are we not the captains of our own ship, and the masters of our own destinies? The answer that the Bible gives us is "no." *He* is the potter, and *we* are the clay.

In the 1961 French film *Leon Morin, Priest*, a young woman claiming to be an atheist decides to play a prank upon a priest. She walks into a confessional booth one afternoon and says, "Forgive me, Father, for I have sinned... I wish to confess that I do not believe in you. I am an atheist."

The young priest is completely unfazed, and in response, he invites her to meet with him in his office the next day to discuss the matter in more detail. And sure enough, she shows up. At one point in their conversation, he pulls out a piece of paper and a pen and asks her if he may draw her portrait. She is flattered and intrigued.

Then he draws a large circle on the page with a small dot in its center. He says to her, pointing to the circle, "This is God," and pointing to the little dot, "this is you. Your problem is that you've been getting the two confused."

Deep down inside, we all know that this is true about us, too. Jeremiah was boldly reminded about this fact on the day he saw the potter at work on his wheel, mending a broken pot.

God is indeed a mender, a spirit who causes the broken shards of our lives to take on meaning and purpose. Is there a place in your own life where the pottery has become cracked? *It is there—and not in the strong places of your world—that I suspect you will soon know God to be at work.*

Let us close with a collect:

> "O God, the strength of the weak and the comfort of sufferers: Mercifully accept our prayers, and grant to us the help of your power, that our sickness may be turned into health, our fear into courage, and our sorrow into joy; through Jesus Christ our Savior. Amen."

THE BEST ANTI-VENOM YOU CAN'T BUY (SEPTEMBER 14, 2013)

"So Moses made a bronze snake and put it up on a pole. Then when anyone was bitten by a snake and looked at the bronze snake, they lived." (Numbers 21:9)

Today we celebrate what is known as Holy Cross Day. It is a day in the church calendar when we remember and focus our attention upon the cross. The date itself is tied the founding of the Church of the Holy Sepulcher in Jerusalem in the 4th Century, where Emperor Constantine's mother, St. Helena, built a church upon a hill that is thought to be that of Golgotha, where our Lord was crucified. It is among the most famous and significant churches in the whole world, for obvious reasons.

Deirdre and I traveled there six years ago with my family, and it is without a doubt one the most fascinating spots I have ever visited. I know that some of you have been there too and can attest to its splendor. We saw Christians from all over the world and from denominations of all sorts, all of us gathered together in that sacred space, each in our own way seeking to venerate and more deeply appreciate that most profound event that is the defining feature of our faith: the cross of Christ.

My goal this morning is to help all of us think about the cross afresh. It is an unfathomably deep and complex thing to consider, as it should be—the idea that God took upon Himself the sins of the whole world, thereby establishing peace between humans and God, once and for all. Today I wish to draw to your attention to just one particular aspect of this inexhaustible event, by focusing on a piece of famous Old Testament scripture that is referenced (somewhat subtly) in our Gospel lesson.

Jesus said, "And I, when I am lifted up from the earth, will draw all people to myself." And then the writer adds, *"He said this to indicate the kind of death he was to die."* In a straightforward sense, we are being told of the encroaching crucifixion, when Jesus was nailed to the cross and then hoisted into the air, being displayed as a deterrent, while the appointed Roman centurions waited for him to breathe his last. He was indeed "lifted up."

But these words "lifted up" also reference an earlier passage in the third chapter of John's Gospel, when Jesus tells Nicodemus: *"And just as Moses lifted up the serpent in the wilderness, so must the Son of Man be lifted up, that whoever believes in him may have eternal life."*

Now bear with me for a moment longer, because I want to talk about what it means for us to be told, "Just as Moses lifted up the serpent in the wilderness, so must the Son of Man be lifted up." What, you may ask, is being referred to here, in this more extended appropriation of the words "lifted up?" I wonder if you get the reference to Moses lifting up the serpent in the wilderness? Before I tell you about it, let me show you something.

This is a painting by Hans Holbein (the younger), called *An Allegory of the Old and New Testaments.* It was painted in 1530, and it hangs in the Scottish National Gallery in Edinburgh. In it, on one side we see Adam and Eve, and Moses receiving the Ten Commandments. Then we find Isaiah and John the Baptist both talking with this 'everyman' at the center of the painting, an individual who represents you and me. They are both pointing at the cross (on the right), where we also see the Virgin Mary, and Christ exiting the tomb, trampling a skeleton under foot and carrying a cross that greatly resembles the one we carried down the aisle just a few moments ago. But there is also *this* in the middle of the left panel: a strange pole with a giant snake wrapped around it. Notice there are people at its base, looking up at it.

Now here is a similar piece from the artist Lucas Cranach. This one hangs above the altar in the main Lutheran church in Weimar, Germany. It covers much of the same material. Notice here, in the background, this same snake on a pole.

Finally, you probably recognize this one: it's a detail from the Sistine Chapel. Notice right here, too, we see the same thing again: a pole with a large serpent wrapped around its shaft. (I'm starting to feel like Dan Brown.) You see that this image is present in the annals of Christian art, and it spans both sides of the Reformation divide.

It comes from a somewhat obscure passage in book of Numbers, where we are told about a very strange occurrence. When the people of Israel became agitated after many years of wandering about in the wilderness, they cursed God, and He, apparently, became angry with them. So God sent out venomous snakes into their tents, which soon led to a rash of deadly snakebites in the camp. When that happened, Moses prayed to God, asking Him to take away the snakes. To this, the Lord said (quote):

> "'Make a snake and put it up on a pole; anyone who is bitten can look at it and live.' So Moses made a bronze snake and put it up on a pole. Then, when anyone was bitten by a snake and looked at the bronze snake, they lived."

This is considered to be the greatest piece of Crucifixion fore-shadowing to be found in the entire Old Testament. Clearly, these artists, along with Jesus himself, felt that a crucial aspect of the cross's impact was anticipated by these events. So what is it?

The people who looked at the brazen serpent on the pole found that, in spite of their fatal bites, they could live. The poison's effect was somehow neutralized. I'm reminded of that great scene in the movie *True Grit*, when Jeff Bridges saves young Mattie Ross's life by sucking the rattlesnake poison out of her wrist. Jesus viewed the event of the cross to serve a similar purpose. He drew the poison that rots our souls unto himself, so that we, too, might live unencumbered by that which would otherwise drag us down.

Notice that Moses' prayer did not result in the disappearance of all of the snakes. The people still were bitten. God rarely answers prayers by removing the snake that causes you to call upon Him. But He also provided an avenue by which they could live in spite of their difficulties.

Perhaps you have experienced this dynamic to be at play in your own life. I wonder if you have ever known the snake bite of this fallen world. May I ask, what is it that is currently holding you down? ...or waking you up? What is it that is currently killing you?

Well, know this, no matter what it is, God's grace is the antidote, and He shed enough of it on Calvary that we can all find collective refuge there. The cross is the place where evil, in its effects, is disarmed and brought under the reign of God's sovereignty. The cross is a place of healing and redemption. In spite of all that ails you, you need only look to it to find the way forward. As St. Paul reminds us, *"nothing can separate us [separate you and me] from the love of God."*

So let us lift high the cross, stumble as we may. In so doing we will also find the way of actual hope that God has prepared in advance for us to walk in. *Amen.*

WORTHINESS IS OVERRATED
(OCT 5, 2013)

*"So you also, when you have done all that you were
ordered to do, say, 'We are worthless slaves; we have
done only what we ought to have done!'" (Luke 17:10)*

Let me open with a question: What jumped out at you from
this morning's readings? ...Not much? Me too. If you feel
that way, don't feel bad. I had the same experience, at least
initially. This morning's lectionary readings are what I would
call a tad inaccessible (and even perhaps somewhat hum-
drum). This is a good thing and as it should be. If it were
up to me to choose which bits of the Bible I want to preach
from each week, you would all suffer. You would hear me
preaching the same sermon each week, and I would gravitate
toward the same types of passages *ad nauseam*. This is one of
the virtues of the lectionary. It challenges us to stretch our
wings a bit.

In a larger sense, this is what's great about Scripture in general. It forces us to engage with ideas that we do not normally encounter in our day-to-day walk. In effect, it lures us to think outside of the box—outside of *our* box, which is especially good for us, since most of us tend to be pretty sure about what we think and about what we like and don't like. We spend a lot of time in life avoiding things that would otherwise challenge us.

And so it is today with the parable found in our Gospel lesson. It is known traditionally as "the parable of the unworthy servant." Our translation is especially tough because it chooses to translate the Greek word for "bondservant" (*doulos*) as "slave," which is a most off-putting word. Most translations, including the classic King James, go with "servant" instead of "slave" for obvious reasons, since it's also accurate and slightly more palatable. The exact meaning of the word lies somewhere between the two.

The parable itself speaks of a rather presumptuous farmhand who works at a large estate with many other people. One day, he comes in from doing his chores and announces that he thinks he deserves the same treatment as the owner of the estate.

Picture *Downton Abbey* for a second. Imagine if suddenly one of the footmen tried to sit down at the dinner table next to Lord Grantham on the evening when the Duchess of Crownington-on-Thisby comes to supper. It would be absolutely scandalous, right?

Or going back in the pop culture canon a bit, do any of you remember the movie from 1984 called *Supergirl?* It's really weak, a notoriously un-compelling superhero movie, which stars a young actress that I hope none of you can name, called Helen Slater, who plays Superman's sister. In one of its dullest moments, we learn about her experience at boarding school.

But *Supergirl*, the movie, is known for one thing: do you know who else stars in *Supergirl* alongside of Helen Slater? That's right: Peter O'Toole, the famous and hugely loved British actor who played Lawrence of Arabia and starred in countless great films.

Or maybe you remember the really obscure horror movie from the early 70s called *The Legend of the Seven Golden Vampires*? Tell me you don't. It stars the amazing horror movie actor Peter Cushing, who is most well-known for playing Dr. Frankenstein and Van Helsing. In this movie, he goes to China and is forced to act alongside seven young Kung-Fu stars who can barely even pronounce the English lines they've been given. Watching him onscreen creates an incredibly lop-sided experience for the viewer, since the caliber of acting feels so mismatched.

Well, that is the type of image Jesus brings to our attention in the Parable of the Unworthy Servant. Imagine if every new wannabe actor who moved to LA felt that they deserved a starring role across from Anthony Hopkins. It would reflect a tremendous lack of perspective, would it not? Just because a person can cry on cue and memorize a few lines doesn't mean they necessarily deserve an Academy Award, right?

Well, that is the point Jesus is trying to make. The problem with his analogy is that in it, you and I are the actors who have completely lost perspective. He's concerned that we may have begun to *overvalue* ourselves at the expense of *undervaluing* him. In the description he offers, the servant has developed a nasty sense of entitlement.

I wonder if you have you ever encountered a person who struggles with a sense of entitlement, a person who thinks too highly of himself or herself? Usually entitlement manifests itself in the form of becoming insensitive to the needs and concerns of others. Entitled people view themselves as distinct and not "normal," as exceptional and not "just like everyone else." According to Jesus, when that happens, people begin to lose their grip on life. They are in desperate need of humility, but that's also the last thing they are inclined to seek out for themselves.

If you can understand these ideas, then perhaps you can also see why it is that passages like this are not all that famous. The Parable of the Unworthy Servant comes at us as a kind of attitude adjustment. Say what you will about yourself and your own degree of humility, but this passage seems to assume that you need more of it. In order to get there, it is suggested to us, all of us, with me at the front of the line, that we stop entertaining the part of our brain that thinks we deserve anything.

So let me ask, would that really be such a bad thing? Imagine that you didn't deserve anything at all. How would that make you feel? What would cross through your mind, for example, on Christmas morning, if you discovered a bunch of gifts under the tree with your name on them? Would that not be a most fantastic surprise? You certainly would not have written out a list for Santa.

The truth is that you *are* the person I'm describing, whether you feel like it or not. You do not deserve rewards for being good. Being good is, after all, its own reward. That's just how we're supposed to be. It should be routine. But it's not, is it? We're not always good, and we spend most of our time thinking about ourselves.

The amazing thing about the Gospel message is that it tells us, to our great amusement, that God's compassion for us is not contingent upon our good behavior; instead, it's born out of the compassion He has for us in spite of our bad behavior. It is His property "always to have mercy." As long as you stay wrapped up in the earning game, which is entitlement writ large, you will miss out on seeing God for who He really is.

Think for a moment of all the people and things that you love. If your house were on fire, what would you try to save? The things that come to mind are just a tip of the iceberg of the things that you have to be grateful to God for, the ways that you have been blessed. We are gathered here this morning, partly in an attempt to thank God in exactly that kind of way.

Even though we are "unworthy," we are invited to share in community with Him and with each other. And He invites us to sit at His table this morning, to eat His bread and drink His wine, and to see if doing so doesn't cause us to feel better about our lives, refreshed and encouraged and, perhaps, even filled with gratitude. *Amen.*

How to Become a Saint without Really Trying

(All Saints' Day, 2013)

"To all God's beloved... who are called to be saints."
(Romans 1:7)

Today is The Feast of All Saints, and I want to talk to you about sainthood. The word "saint" does not mean what many people think it means. If you look at the Biblical account, for example, (St.) Paul calls all the members of the church saints. Romans opens: *"To all God's beloved in Rome, who are called to be saints: Grace to you and peace from God our Father and the Lord Jesus Christ."*

Christians are, by definition, saints. This is because we believe that God sees the perfect righteousness of Christ when He looks upon His flock.

That means that today is a day when we are called for a moment to think about the huge breadth of the body of Christ, of whom we are but a tiny part.

There are over 7,000 Episcopal churches in the US, with over 2 million members, and over 80 million Anglicans worldwide.

Furthermore, there are estimated to be approximately 2.18 billion Christians in the entire world, which makes up almost a third of the Earth's population!

But that's not all: look at the painting by the amazing Albrecht Dürer on the cover of your bulletin. It depicts not only the saints on earth, but also all of the multitude of saints in heaven, who have gone before us. *All* Saints' Day affirms the fundamental Christian belief that there is a prayerful spiritual bond between those in heaven (the "Church triumphant"), and the living (the "Church militant"), and today we remember and, in some sense, join with them.

A conservative estimate of Christians who have lived and died in the last 2000 years suggests at least 14 billion. Just thinking about it is pretty mind-boggling, and you can see why we do it. It offers a really helpful, reorienting perspective. As one person put it, "I'm not much, but I'm all I think about." Well, All Saints' Day obliterates that kind of self-absorption.

Saints in our tradition are not the holy people we tend to envision. It is a not a term that refers just to some tiny minority of extra-spiritual human beings who walk(ed) the earth, hovering about three inches above the ground. I'm sure you know people who exude extreme serenity and detachment, who seem extra-spiritual. Of course they are not to be discounted and are fully included in the ranks of saints… but focusing on their personal qualities of transcendent personality is not what sainthood is about.

You see, in Christianity, saints are not holy people in the sense that we typically think of; they are simply people who acknowledge their *unholiness* before a perfect God, putting their trust in Him instead of in themselves. William Porcher Dubose put it like this: "Only the saint knows sin." Being a saint has as much to do with knowing that you are *not* God as it does with anything else.

If we look at the Bible, for example, we do not actually find a very impressive group of people described. In fact, quite the opposite is the case: we find a bunch of really flawed people, a lot of interesting people, full of mistake-making tendencies (in spite of their good intentions)... but we do find the story of a very impressive *God*, who loved those people and made them the object of His affection.

Of course, the Bible does tell the story of one otherworldly, exceptionally holy man. That is Jesus. He was unendingly compassionate and hugely patient. He saw the truth behind the world's lies. He never let exhaustion overcome his ability to be there for the sake of others. He connected with people of all ages and never let fear run the show in his life. He lived a life full of prayer and mindfulness, and he preached sermons that have never been topped (like the one in today's lesson). He had holy powers and was able to heal the sick, and even raise the dead to life!

Next to him, though, in the Bible, there is not a single person who even comes close! The rest of the people described are like Swiss cheese, in that they are full of holes.

The classic example is that of St. Peter. Truth be told, he was far less impressive than the current pope, if you compare their records. Peter is the one who doubted his faith and subsequently sank. He is the one who tried to talk Jesus out of going to the cross. He fell asleep in the Garden of Gethsemane, after he was asked to stay awake. Most famously, Peter denied Christ three times. After that, he ran to the tomb, but John beat him in their little footrace. He then subsequently led the entire Christian church astray, as Paul put it, "out of line with the Gospel." And finally, Peter ran from persecution in Rome, only returning after he was confronted by the risen Christ on the Appian Way. Does this affirm or challenge your idea of what it means to be a saint?

But here's the thing about Peter. He got one thing right. He said to Jesus, "You are truly the Son of God." …And *that* was enough for him to become Jesus' very own delegate as the leader of the Church. Can you imagine harder shoes to fill? But that was God's point, which we are here to be reminded of today.

You see, God loved Peter and used him anyway. He made him great in spite of his problems. And Peter did do some great things, some brave things. Most notably, he was able to admit when he was wrong, which is a most saintly quality indeed. Plus, he gave God the credit for all of the good things that he was able to accomplish.

Luther described the life of the Christian with the following Latin phrase: *simul iustus et peccator*, which means, "saint and sinner simultaneously." To his way of thinking, the two were not mutually exclusive. I think it rings true to life, don't you? Not "saint *or* sinner" but "saint *and* sinner," a mixed bag, in whom the Spirit of God is at work. This should come as a great comfort for two reasons:

First, because if you aren't feeling very holy and are thinking you should be, then rest assured, you've come to the right place, which really means, to the right God.

Second, because it means that God is indeed in the midst of doing amazing things with and through little old you. Do your kids think you hung the moon even though you know yourself to be lacking in so many areas of life? Or maybe you've found yourself to be a way better mom than you ever thought you would be. Perhaps you have even impressed yourself at some point, by doing something uncharacteristically selfless for the sake of simply helping a friend in need.

I am struck this morning by the beauty of the flower arrangements that adorn our altar. Our Flower Guild is so inspiring. They are both a concrete expression of what I've been describing, and also—perhaps more importantly—a metaphor for the wondrous things that God chooses to do through normal Christian people. I, for one, am most encouraged by their example. *Amen.*

STUFFING THE TURKEY WITH PROZAC (NOV 6, 2013)

> *"For I have come to turn a man against his father, a daughter against her mother, a daughter-in-law against her mother-in-law— a man's enemies will be the members of his own household..." (Matthew 10:35-36)*

This passage tends to make people very uncomfortable: *hating fathers, mothers, sisters and brothers...* As one lady I spoke with earlier in the week commented, "It doesn't sound much like Jesus."

A similar, but more expanded version, of this same statement is found in Matthew's Gospel:

> "Do not suppose that I have come to bring peace to the earth. I did not come to bring peace, but a sword. For I have come to turn 'a man against his father, a daughter against her mother, a daughter-in-law against her mother-in-law—a man's enemies will be the members of his own household' (Matt 10:34-7)."

Can you believe it? "I did not come to bring peace, but a sword"?!

Allow me to suggest that the thing that makes us uncomfortable about these passages is not so much the idea of a sword over and above peace. Sure, that's a factor. But I think the primary thing that makes us uncomfortable here is the portrait he gives of where the sword does its cutting: the family. After all, familial unrest is a very uncomfortable thing.

But is it so uncommon? You would think from the way people react to this passage that they've never experienced any disagreements with the members of their family. Have you really never seen, to paraphrase, "a daughter-in-law against her mother-in-law"? Perhaps you've heard the joke: What's the difference between outlaws and in-laws? Outlaws are "*wanted.*"

My point is that family strife is common rather than uncommon, and Jesus had no illusions about that. There's a *New Yorker* cartoon that shows a woman stuffing a turkey while talking to a friend. The caption reads: "This year I'm going to make sure we have a happy Thanksgiving... so I'm stuffing the turkey with Prozac." It's the same point. Two thousand years later, this material still has traction.

So where do Jesus' words cut against the grain? Sure, he exposes a rather embarrassing reality that tarnishes many family situations, but what does he challenge in doing so? The answer, I think, is straightforward: he is challenging "the primacy of family."

The primacy of family is a no-brainer in Southern culture, but you find it most anywhere. One portrayal of this idea that sticks in my mind comes from the show *The Wire*, which takes place in Baltimore. On multiple occasions the criminal mastermind, Barksdale, was seen spouting off lines like: "We're fam-ly, fam-ly! Blood is thicker than water, son." But this understanding of the primacy of family was no less present in the Ancient Near-East, where Jesus first uttered these counter-cultural claims.

The truth is simply that Jesus was not as enamored of The Nuclear Family as most people are. We see this not only in his teaching on the subject but in his personal life, too. Keep in mind, he never married or had any natural-born children. We see the deposits of this thinking in the life of St. Paul as well.

All of this begs the question: Is it possible that we *over*value family? Or that we value family at the expense of valuing our neighbors? Jesus seemed to think so, and he contended as much in a famous passage from Matthew's Gospel:

"While Jesus was still talking to the crowd, his mother and brothers stood outside, wanting to speak to him. Someone told him, 'Your mother and brothers are standing outside, wanting to speak to you.' He replied to him, 'Who is my mother, and who are my brothers?' Pointing to his disciples, he said, 'here are my mother and my brothers. For whoever does the will of my Father in heaven is my brother and sister and mother.'"

Do you see what this shows us? It wasn't that he was against "family;" He was all for it, but he had a much more expansive vision of what that single word could mean. In other words, *Jesus was more taken with the idea of treating people that are not part of your family as though they were.* He touted the importance, for example, of forgiving enemies and of loving the outsider. Christ's vision in this sense was expansive and inclusive, rather than exclusive. And the fruit of this vision? It's us.

Make no mistake, church *is* family. Christians have the common bond of a shared eternity, the reach of which extends forever. I'll close with the words of St. Paul: *"He has given us the spirit of adoption, that we might be heirs of his eternal glory."*

Amen.

FOR GOD'S SAKE (NOV 17, 2013)

"Then he said to them, 'Nation will rise against nation, and kingdom against kingdom; there will be great earthquakes, and in various places famines and plagues; and there will be dreadful portents and great signs from heaven... This will give you an opportunity to testify.'"
(Luke 21:10-11, 13)

In this morning's Gospel lesson, Jesus offers us a jarring image of the world we live in. As we wait for him to come again, we are told to not be surprised when wars break out, or when we encounter massive natural disasters like the recent typhoon which has gutted portions of the Philippines. Similarly we are warned about famines, where huge amounts of people will be found to live in poverty, in need of decent food and proper healthcare.

On top of all that, we are also told that on a more personal level, we Christians will experience persecution for our beliefs. Jesus says that the hope we profess will arouse ambivalence and cultural dissent.

And so it is. Can anyone deny these claims? Those who first heard him speak these words heard in them an element of prophecy. But just forty years after he spoke them, the Temple in Jerusalem was burned by Roman troops at the command of Emperor Titus. The city was devastated. It is fair to suggest that after those tragic events in 70 AD, Jesus' words took on a descriptive, rather than a predictive, tone. They were no longer understood to describe events that were anticipated. Instead, they naturally mapped onto the world that people saw all around them.

And none of us are strangers to these aspects of life on Earth, are we? We live in a fallen world, where it often seems like strife is the norm, both from within and without. Let us not kid ourselves about that. It is helpful to note that the Bible does not apply a minimizing, glossy veneer to the reality of suffering.

But if our listening stops there, then we miss the most important part of his words. For he says, all of this "will give you an opportunity to testify." We are told that in the face of worldly hardship, the Christian life makes a difference. This is because the Christian life is a life of love, hope, and service. Christianity sees in unrest an opportunity to provide help and comfort. It sees in un-surety a time to trust in God's grace. It sees in devastation a need for prayer and engagement.

So let me ask: is there anywhere in your life where it seems like the fallen world is beating at your door? Are you in the midst of a fresh encounter with suffering? We are encouraged by our Lord to endure and not to bury our heads in the sand. Let us rise to such occasions, literally for God's sake. We close with the prayer of St. Francis:

> Lord, make me an instrument of Thy peace;
> Where there is hatred, let me sow love;
> Where there is injury, pardon;
> Where there is error, truth;
> Where there is doubt, faith;
> Where there is despair, hope;
> Where there is darkness, light;
> And where there is sadness, joy.
> O Divine Master, Grant that I may not so much
>   seek
> To be consoled as to console;
> To be understood as to understand;
> To be loved as to love.
> For it is in giving that we receive;
> It is in pardoning that we are pardoned;
> And it is in dying that we are born to eternal life.

Amen.

AND FOR DESSERT: BITTERSWEET
SCROLL (NOV 24, 2013)

"Then I looked, and I saw a hand stretched out to me.
In it was a scroll, which he unrolled before me. On both
sides of it were written words of lament and mourning
and woe... Then he said to me, 'Son of man, eat this
scroll I am giving you and fill your stomach with it.' So
I ate it, and it tasted as sweet as honey in my mouth."
(Ezekiel 2:9-10, 3:3)

This morning is Christ the King Sunday, which I find to
be somewhat confusing. Certainly it can be a misleading to
think of God in this way—as a king—for we are inclined,
immediately upon hearing that word, to think of kingly attributes like *triumph* and *victory* and *conquest*. We envision
throne-sitting and *strength*, *iron rule* and *authority*, which is
to say that we quickly get off-track. But today's readings help
to keep us from getting the wrong idea. They give us a very
different picture of what it means for Christ to be our king.

In the Gospel lesson, we see a king who loses willingly to the
ways of the world. His way of doing things is met with cruci-

fixion, which is to say, it is decisively rejected. For his disciples, the only initial reaction that they found in these events was despair. They saw a failed campaign, a conquest that had come to nothing. Three years of their lives had been given over to serving a lost cause. Now they needed to do a massive amount of re-grouping. Success was the last thing on their minds.

I emphasize this aspect of the reading in an attempt draw out an important point: *our triumphalistic hopes do not find affirmation in the Christian story.* In fact, quite the opposite is the case. In this story, they are squashed. It is as the prophet Isaiah was told by God: "My thoughts are not your thoughts, nor are your ways my ways."

And so the notion of Christ's reign brings with it a redefining element. Words like "glory" and "hope" and "blessing" and "rescue" find very different explanations in *his* kingdom. When our ideas of those words meet his ideas of them, our ideas ricochet back at us like bullets that God has chosen to deflect. One amusing example of this idea is found in a cartoon that came out a few years ago. It depicts Daniel in the lions' den. The rather sarcastic caption reads, "God has a wonderful plan for your life." If Christ on the cross is meant to be viewed as a portrait of glory—and it is—then it is also the case that God is *not so much in the business of wish-fulfillment as He is in the business of wish-deconstruction.*

You see, faith is indeed a thing that blesses us primarily by *un*doing us (and not the other way around). I was listening to an interview with a Lutheran pastor, Nadia Bolz-Weber, yesterday. In it she described how they make use of a variety of different liturgies at her church in Denver. The equivalent for Episcopalians is something that we try to do here at Grace, which is using various Eucharistic services from the *Book of Common Prayer* rather than just one particular strand. We don't just do *Rite 1*, or only *Rite 2 Prayer A*. We use *Rite 1* (as you'll see this Thursday if you can make it), and we use *Rite 2 A* (as we're doing this morning), and we use *Rite 2B* and *2C* and *2D*, not to mention emphasizing many of the services and Feast Days that punctuate our church calendar (like this morning). This approach, by the way, was new to me when I arrived here a year ago. I had only ever experienced services that were committed to a single form of worship, week in and week out.

Here is what Bolz-Weber had to say about this aspect of worship at her own church: "as an inclusive parish, we use all kinds of liturgy… not so that everyone will be made comfortable, but so that everyone will be made equally *un*-comfortable." She conveys a deep grasp of the way that God often blesses us most by throwing us off our stride.

Two years ago late-night talk show host Conan O'Brian gave the commencement address at Dartmouth College. You may remember that he was given the Tonight Show for a brief period of time, only to have it taken away from him and given back to Jay Leno by the network. It was on the heels of those events, about a year and a half later, that he had these words to say:

> "By definition, Commencement speakers at an Ivy League college are considered successful. But a little over a year ago, I experienced a profound and very public disappointment. I did not get what I wanted, and I left

a system that had nurtured and helped define me for the better part of seventeen years. I went from being in the center of the grid to not only off the grid, but underneath the coffee table that the grid sits on, lost in the shag carpeting that is underneath the coffee table supporting the grid. It was the making of a career disaster...

"But then something spectacular happened. Fog-bound, with no compass, and adrift, I started trying things. I grew a strange, cinnamon beard. I dove into the world of social media and started tweeting my comedy. I threw together a national tour. I played the guitar, did stand-up, wore a skin-tight blue leather suit, recorded an album, made a documentary, and frightened my friends and family.

"Ultimately, I abandoned all preconceived perceptions of my career path... I did a lot of silly, unconventional, spontaneous and seemingly irrational things, and guess what—with the exception of the blue leather suit, *it was the most satisfying and fascinating year of my professional life.* To this day I still don't understand exactly what happened, but I have never had more fun, been more challenged, and this is important—had more conviction about what I was doing.

"How could this be true? It's simple: there are few things more liberating in this life than having your worst fear realized, and your path at 22 will not necessarily be your path at 32 or 42. One's dream is constantly evolving, rising and falling, changing course... It is our failure to become our perceived ideal that ultimately defines us and makes us unique. It's not easy, but if you accept your misfortune and handle it right, your perceived failure can be a catalyst for profound re-invention."

Though Conan doesn't phrase things in Christian terms, he does a beautiful job of describing that element of life which faith embraces. As one person put it, "The quickest way around is through." It is the way of the cross. This morning we come before a God of whom St. Paul said, "He has rescued us from the power of darkness and transferred us into *the kingdom of his beloved Son*." He has done this not by giving us our dreams, but rather by lovingly denying them, so that we might discover God's dream for us.

I wonder if you are feeling the screws turn in your own life at the moment. Where is it that disaster appears to be looming? Where is there pressure building? Know that it is in that place more than others in your life that I suspect God to be doing something important and compassionate, something which you will ultimately come to value.

In one of my favorite passages of Scripture, the prophet Ezekiel is told by God to "eat a scroll" that is "covered in words of woe." Initially, the taste is bitter. But to the prophet's great surprise, he soon finds that the bitter flavors are replaced by the sweetness of honey. "Glory" and "hope" and "blessing" and "rescue" are things that only ever truly come from God. And they often come to us like that scroll in Ezekiel; they taste bitter going down, yet turn out to be full of profound and lasting sweetness. Only the greatest of kings ever could have thought to issue an edict such as this.

Amen.

16402573R00157

Made in the USA
Middletown, DE
13 December 2014